Developing Deacon-Led Ministry Teams

Meeting Needs Through
Discovering and Using Spiritual Gifts

Charles Garner
John Temple
Keith Wilkinson

Developing Deacon-Led Ministry Teams

ISBN: 979-8-9924408-1-2

Acknowledgements:

Scripture references are from the English Standard Version, the New American Standard Version (1977), and the King James Version. Any others are noted in the text.

Contributors:

To the deacons in the churches we have served across the nation—your humble ministry made you true partners in the service of God. Among them are our fathers and friend: Charles H. "Red" Garner, a Baptist deacon with a servant's heart; Dr. Bill Burkett, who embodied the true spirit of service; and Guy Wilkinson—Christian, deacon, and humble servant.

Special thanks to my friend, Aurelius Vale—without his editorial partnership, this book would not be in your hands.

Just as iron sharpens iron,
friends sharpen the minds of each other.
Proverbs 27:17 Contemporary English Version

About the Authors:

Charles Garner is an author, curriculum designer, and teacher to the church. His calling is to equip the saints for the work of ministry. He has authored, edited, or designed over fifty-five resources and books for use in the Christian community. His works include *Gifts of Grace*, *Teaching to Make a Difference*, *Reclaiming the Real Jesus* (co-authored with Dr. Ivan Parke), *Thinking of Leaving*, *Beyond Expectations*, and *Profiles from Paul*. His latest work is *It's NOT Adam's Fault!*.

Dr. John Temple has served as a church business administrator, minister of education, and pastor. He is a seasoned consultant in deacon ministry, church administration, Sunday School, and discipleship. His passion in ministry is mobilizing God's people for meaningful service. In addition to *Developing Deacon-Led Ministry Teams*, he is the author of *Unleashing the Power of Deacon-Led Ministry Teams*, which explores the untapped potential within in local congregations.

Keith Wilkinson, in addition to his pastoral leadership, has served as a Sunday School consultant with the Baptist Sunday School Board, as Director of the Sunday School Department for the Mississippi Baptist Convention, and as Director of Sunday School Ministries for the Oklahoma Baptist Convention. He has authored numerous leadership articles and is a respected conference leader, often featured at training events across the nation. Through his leadership, he has influenced the ministries of countless churches and impacted the spiritual growth of millions of followers of Christ.

Table of Contents

Introduction

Deacon ministry has always been a dynamic part of church life. From the initial group of men selected in Acts 6, deacons have served as partners in ministry with pastors and key leaders in the church. Over the centuries, deacons have provided leadership and ministry to congregations both great and small. Regardless of the size or complexity of a church's ministry, deacons have consistently been an integral component of effective ministry.

The dilemma has never been the existence of deacons—but rather their function.

The question is: *What are deacons supposed to do?*

Some believe deacons should function as an administrative board—reviewing and approving plans and proposals. Some churches see the deacon body as an honor guard that meets regularly, discusses much, but performs little. Others have proposed that deacons are to be pastoral ministers in some fashion. Many deacons, dedicated to being the best they can be for the Lord, often express frustration—and sometimes guilt—when confronted with expectations that imply all deacons are to serve in the same way.

A recent trend in deacon ministry is the **team ministry** approach. In this model, deacons identify several specific ministries that the deacon body will perform. Each deacon is assigned to—or chooses—one of these ministry areas. With the diversity of ministries and the specific focus upon one function, deacons often serve with greater motivation, satisfaction, and success.

While this approach is an improvement, questions remain—especially when assignments don't match a deacon's preference, interest, or ability. One key dynamic is often overlooked: the **spiritual gifts** that God has given to each believer.

"The manifestation of the Spirit is given to every man to profit withal.... But now hath God set the members every one of them in the body, as it hath pleased him... but God hath tempered the body together..."
—1 Corinthians 12:7, 18, 24

"As every man hath received the gift, even so minister the same one to another as good stewards of the manifold grace of God."
—1 Peter 4:10

God has given every Christian (including deacons) certain gifts—spiritual gifts, or more accurately, *grace gifts*. These gifts equip us for individual ministries, and together, empower the whole Body to fulfill its calling. When we serve in alignment with the gifts God has placed in us, our joy increases, our power is renewed, and our ministries bear greater fruit.

This book provides a guide for discovering those gifts and applying them in real-life ministry through **deacon-led ministry teams**. As you explore the content ahead, pray that God will reveal to you the specific ministry He has prepared for you—in and through the Body of Christ.

Session 1

The Development of Deacon Ministry

Deacon ministry has gone through an evolutionary process in Protestant churches. Knowing the development of deacon ministry will help us know where we are in our understanding of deacon ministry and help us identify improvements we can make to serve Christ more effectively.

Evolving Concepts of Deacon Service

The New Testament does not list specific duties for deacons. The focus is on deacon qualifications rather than specific responsibilities. Without firm biblical guidelines for service, differing concepts regarding the deacons' work have developed. Let's do a quick scan of several approaches that have been deployed.

Deacons as Board of Directors

Sometimes the term "board of deacons" has been used to refer to deacons. The concept of a "board" developed in the late 1800's. Business problems began to be discussed by groups of persons in an effort to find acceptable solutions. Often these groups met for a meal around a wooden or board table to discuss their problems. A group of persons charged with decision making became known as a "board." Governing groups were known as a "board of directors" or "board of trustees."

As deacons assumed much of the management of church properties and finances in the late 1800's, the concept of "board of directors" was, unfortunately, transferred to the church.

Dr. Howard Foshee in *The Ministry of the Deacon* gives some evidences that deacons are operating under the concept of a board. Deacons are operating as a board...

(1) when all major recommendations from church organizations and church committees are screened by the deacons to determine whether they should go to the congregation.

(2) when the pastor and staff members are directly responsible to the deacons rather than to the church.

(3) when the use or expenditure of major church resources, such as facilities and finances, must first be approved by the deacons.

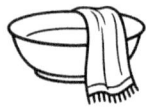

How many of these factors reveal that deacons serve as a board of directors in your church?

How do you feel about that role for deacons?

Several Protestant churches have no levels of authority above the local congregation. These churches are autonomous, making decisions in a more-or-less democratic process. The congregation, under the leadership of the Holy Spirit, makes final decisions. Deacon authority, then, is a matter of Christian influence rather than designated authority as in a board of directors.

Churches make a mistake when they adopt the term "board of deacons." No scriptural basis for this concept exists. Such a concept is in direct conflict with the congregational form of government followed in most of these non-hierarchical churches.

Deacons as Business Managers

Some persons view deacons as church business managers. Some note Acts 6:3 as their biblical authority—*Look ye out among you seven men...whom we may appoint over this business*. It is important to note that the passage states *whom we may appoint over **this** business* rather than **the** business. The word, *this,* refers to the immediate need facing the Jerusalem church at that particular time—the crisis of the distribution to widows.

How did the concept of deacons as business managers emerge?

In reaction to Catholic church structures during the Reformation, John Calvin began to speak of the deacon as a layman rather than as a member of the clergy as had been the case in the Catholic church. He taught that deacons should serve others—including preaching and ministering to the sick and poor. This servant model was in keeping with the New Testament and was followed for quite some time.

The historic 1774 *Charleston Confession of Faith* initiated a change in the work of deacons. Deacons were instructed to serve at the Lord's table, to collect and dispense aid for the poor, to assist in maintaining the fellowship of the flock, and *to give close attention to relieving the pastor of secular church concerns*. The last point was to influence deacon ministry to a great extent.

R.B.C. Howell in his book, *The Deaconship* (1846), heavily influenced the work of deacons. His premise was that deacons should focus on administering the temporal affairs of the church. Deacons were to take care of the *secular* business of the church—while the pastor tended to the *spiritual* affairs. Many churches assigned responsibilities for all church business to deacons.

In the 1920's Prince E. Burroughs wrote *Honoring the Deaconship*. This book was widely studied and strengthened the idea that deacons were to direct the business affairs of the church.

Dr. Foshee suggests that deacons are operating as church business managers...

(1) when the deacons' responsibilities are composed solely of business management matters.

(2) when the deacons administer the affairs of the church primarily as a business operation.

(3) when deacons are viewed as the decision-makers in all business affairs.

(4) when business efficiency becomes more important than Christian growth and service.

Deacons Serving in Pastoral Ministries

Gaines S. Dobbins, distinguished Southern Baptist professor, probably did more than anyone else to call attention to the spiritual ministry of the deacon. In his book, *Baptist Churches in Action* (1929), Dr. Dobbins called attention to the spiritual qualities deacons should possess. He referred to the deacon as a "specially qualified man of God called by his church to high and holy scriptural office."

Churches began to rethink the work of deacons and a new spiritual dimension began to evolve. The spiritual qualifications for deacons stress the importance of ministering to the needs of persons. Dr. Foshee, in *The Ministry of the Deacon*, stated...

"The deacon is a co-laborer with his pastor in implementing the church's function of ministry. Pastor and deacons stand together as partners in a spiritual task. Together they serve in the pastoral ministries of a church."

He provided an enlarged statement of the deacon's tasks:

(1) Proclaim the gospel to believers and unbelievers.

- Participate in the witnessing activities.
- Participate in the preaching program.

(2) Care for the church's members and other persons in the community.

- Minister in times of crises.

- Provide pastoral counsel and referral.

- Provide vocational guidance.

- Perform acts of benevolence.

(3) Lead the church to engage in a fellowship of worship, witness, education, ministry, and application.

- Maintain church fellowship.

- Lead corporate worship.

- Administer ordinances.

- Be informed about the life and work of church.

- Set a personal example of Christian living.

(4) Lead the church in performing its tasks.

- Interpret the work of the church to church members and the community.

- Encourage cooperative work with other churches.

Dr. Foshee helped move us toward an understanding of a deacon body as a ministering group. The list of responsibilities above is a fairly comprehensive list of deacon involvement in churches.

At least from the 1950's, some churches have implemented a form of "deacon family ministry." The emphasis evolved until the 1960's and 70's when the Church Administration Department of the Baptist Sunday School Board developed the Deacon Family Ministry Plan to help deacons perform ministry along with their pastors to the members of their churches. In this plan of ministry, the church membership is organized by family groups. A number of the families are then assigned to deacons. The ratio is usually 10-15 families per deacon. Each deacon is responsible for ministry to the families under his care.

In this plan of ministry individual deacons visit in the homes of the families assigned to them and minister as needs arise. They minister to families through visits, letters, cards and calls, communicating information to the families as needed. Individual deacons conduct ministry projects with families as planned in deacons' meetings and visit families in crisis experiences. Deacons also submit reports to the appropriate deacon officers.

The Deacon Family Ministry Plan groups the family units of a church uniformly and assigns them to the deacons for ministry. In most churches where the plan has been adopted, it has met with mixed results. Some deacons take the responsibility seriously, some attempt it half-heartedly, while others do nothing but feel guilty because they do not contact their families. Ministry requires more than a mere contact anyway. Most deacons are woefully lacking in the training and skills required to deal with many of the complex problems faced by the families and members of our churches.

Additional works supporting the concept of deacons as ministers have been produced over the last several years. Henry Webb reinforced the ministering role of deacons in his 1980 work entitled *Deacons: Servant Models in the Church*. Training in ministry skills for specific situations was offered by Homer D. Carter in his 1980 book *Equipping Deacons in Caring Skills*.

While these works emphasized the ministering role of deacons, the results, at best, have been less than satisfying.

Moving in Different Directions

Is it wrong for a deacon body to consider some of the business and administrative concerns of the church? No, it isn't. This group of persons should be able to guide the church in its direction of ministry. The opinion of this group provides a good sampling of the general membership. This group should be respected and because of that, their approval of a direction or action should help provide leadership and influence for the church membership.

Is the Deacon Family Ministry Plan off base? Certainly not! Families are in crises today more than ever. Some deacons have a very effective ministry in extending care and counsel to families. Some, however, are ineffectual—even having a sense of failure.

But...

better ways—more biblical ways—of doing ministry can be developed. These approaches employ the principles of servanthood, giftedness, and team ministry to minister more effectively to the needs of a church's membership and community.

Deacon Ministry Teams

A deacon body carries responsibilities of ministry inherent in the servant-leadership role to which they have been called. The designation of deacon (*diakonos*) implies ministry. This word from the New Testament indicates a table waiter, a servant of a master, and eventually a leader in the early church. The word is a compound: *dia* = through; *konos* = dust. Literally, **diakonos** means "***through dust***." The term evokes the image is of a servant hurrying across dusty roads, kicking up a cloud behind him as he runs to do his master's bidding. In essence, a deacon is a servant—a minister of grace in motion.

Although the New Testament doesn't specify duties deacons conduct, the language indicates that service or ministry is at the very heart of being a deacon. Lack of a list of duties might very well be providential. With no definitive parameters, responsibilities are expansive enough to encompass ministry needs as they arise. Every congregation is able to tailor-make deacon roles.

Some churches are discovering that a single-emphasis-approach such as the Deacon Family Ministry Plan does not include the variety of responsibilities required for effective deacon ministry. Individual differences of gifts, personalities, talents and skills often are not considered. It is grossly unfair to expect all persons to respond equally well to the same demand. These churches have developed a system for assigning deacons to ministry teams to perform the tasks needed from deacons.

Team ministry aims toward diversified responsibilities of deacons. The biblical concept of spiritual gifts is the basis for assignment of deacons to specific ministries. God has given each deacon spiritual gifts that equip him or her for a specific ministry. Organizing deacon ministry around spiritual gifts recognizes the diversity and uniqueness of the ministry that God has called each deacon to perform. Instead of approaching deacon ministry from a "cookie-cutter" mentality, deacon ministry for each deacon and each church will be tailored specifically to the gifts that God has given to each deacon and church.

Deacon ministry can include administrative and ministry functions. Emphases such as Deacon Family Ministry Plan can be included. The list and number of ministries will vary according to the needs of a particular church or situation.

Several factors are common to Deacon Ministry Teams:

1. The deacons identify the responsibilities they wish to accept. These responsibilities can be determined either by survey of deacons or survey of church membership.

2. Deacons are assigned to a particular responsibility for a period of time, usually one year.

3. The process of assignment is usually performed by the individual deacons or by deacon officers. Factors such as previous experience, personal interests, and need for the ministry are used in the assignment process.

By developing deacon ministry teams using the spiritual gifts of each deacon, effectiveness and joy in ministry will be realized as God's power flows through the lives of the deacon body.

The next wave in deacon ministry, developing deacon ministry teams, is actually a return to biblical principles and the ministry model of the New Testament church. When freedom, joy and power are seen in the lives of deacons, the church will have a model of ministry and the world will once again stand in awe and wonder as God works through the lives of His people. This book is about using spiritual gifts to form deacons into effective ministering teams.

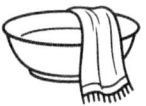 **How many of these factors above are utilized in your deacon ministry to help deacons serve as ministry teams in your church?**

How do you feel about the idea of deacon ministry teams?

Notes and Observations

Session 2

The Role of Deacons in the Modern Church

How a church is organized communicates much of the expectations in the leadership positions of pastor and deacon. The debate over the relationship of pastor and deacon along with the question of the role of the deacon are rooted in our perception of leadership in a church. Since the industrial revolution, our perception typically has been that of deacons as an executive board ruling over all committees and programs. They are administrative problem solvers.

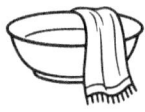 **Draw a diagram of your church's organization including the following positions—pastor, deacons, committees, congregation.**

Compare your drawing to the two following styles of churches and see which style more nearly matches that of your church.

The Typical Church

The typical organization of Protestant churches generally (and certain evangelical churches particularly) is rooted more in the structure of the Catholic church before the reformation and our political democratic system. Just because we are familiar with this style of church organization does not mean that it finds its roots in the New Testament. The following illustration depicts the typical structure in many churches.

Several emphases are evident in the typical church organization:

1. Emphasis on position.

Typically, the roles of pastor and deacon are seen as positions to be occupied. With an emphasis on position comes the question of authority and prestige. The entire issue of ordination and qualifications usually has to do with whether someone "qualifies to be over someone else."

2. Emphasis on spirituality.

The higher up the traditional ladder one climbs, the more "spiritual" they are perceived. This spirituality is not measured by service, but by title and position obtained.

3. Emphasis on authority.

The more "spiritual" one is, the more authority over other people one is assumed to possess. With the emphasis on authority, the focus is removed from God and placed upon power struggles. These struggles are manifest in the selection process as everyone attempts to move up the ladder by defeating someone else for the position.

4. Emphasis on privilege.

The higher the position on the ladder, the greater the privilege assumed. The better parking places and seats of honor are reserved for the ones in power.

5. Emphasis on restricted divine revelation.

In the typical church, only the pastor can receive "a word from God." Because of this restricted source, only projects the pastor wishes to perform are considered priority.

6. Emphasis on uniform ministry from each position.

In the typical church, ministry and services are expected according to the positions honored by the church. No effort is made to discover the unique gifts of various leaders to maximize their service, motivation, and usefulness by God. The common problem in the typical church is that ministry is expected to be performed by the "ordained" of the church. As a result, the fellowship hurts because needs go unanswered while the leadership retreats in weariness or restricts ministry to performing tasks compelled by duty instead of spiritual calling and equipping.

The New Testament Church

In the early New Testament church, the fellowship grew because of an emphasis on servanthood and sacrifice to help others in Jesus name. The following diagram illustrates a structure more in keeping with the New Testament church.

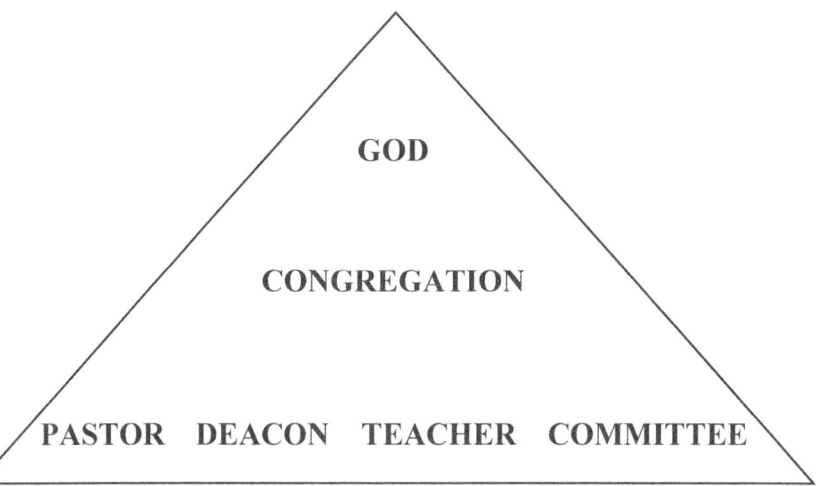

In this illustration, the following emphases are evident:

1. Emphasis on function.

The role of deacon is the function of service. The reason the functions are horizontal instead of vertical is that the emphasis is on a diversity of function, not a debate of authority.

2. Emphasis on service.

Titles such as pastor, deacon, and teacher are descriptions of service being offered by church members, not titles attained. The creation of these ministry roles resulted from God addressing needs in the fellowship through spiritual people who had surrendered their life to Jesus to serve others in His name.

3. Emphasis on a diversity of gifts.

In the New Testament church, it was accepted that God equipped saints for the ministries He intended them to do. A person's spiritual gifts were indicators of the ministry he or she was to perform in the Body of Christ. A diversity of gifts strengthened the church as it attempted to meet a wide range of needs within the fellowship.

4. Emphasis on usefulness.

Everyone was to be useful in the kingdom. The reason one was saved was to serve in the kingdom, not just to be served. Usefulness was revealed in practical love rendered in the name of Jesus.

5. Emphasis on expanded ministry.

The development of a specific ministry in a particular church was dictated by two factors. First, the need of believers dictated the ministry created. Second, the gifts given the believers by the Holy Spirit revealed who would be assigned the responsibility.

6. Emphasis on every member becoming a minister.

One might have entered a church fellowship to be served. However, it was understood that as one matured spiritually, he or she would involve themselves in service. Maturity was revealed in ministry to others and in forgetting self.

Application

The expectations for deacons are different in each of these church structures. In the typical church, the deaconship is considered to be an office to be filled in order to be over the work of the church. In the New Testament church, the deaconship is considered a position of service to meet the needs within the fellowship and community.

The fundamental difference is the foundation of much debate about the role deacons fulfill. This difference must be resolved within a church before any effective and fulfilling ministry can be preformed by a body of deacons. The big question remains: Are deacons administrators or ministers? The following section will help provide a biblical basis for our further discussion of and approach to deacon ministry.

The New Testament Pattern

The New Testament pattern for the church can be seen in the birth of the church found in the book of Acts. When the Spirit filled and baptized those gathered in the upper room of Pentecost, the church was birthed (Acts 2:4; 1 Cor. 12:13). One of the first concerns about the early church might be the size of the church's membership.

The church began with 120 disciples in the upper room and on the first day of existence, 3,000 converts were added. Because of the Holy Spirit's work in the lives of the saints, the Lord added daily to the church (Acts 2:47). For instance, the number of disciples grew to 5000 as a result of Peter's preaching at the Temple. The church grew, literally, by leaps and bounds. Almost overnight, the membership grew to 5,000+ members. By the time of the dispute in Acts 6, it is estimated that the church in Jerusalem had 25,000 members.

A second concern is the organization of the church to handle this fast-growing membership. This exponential growth naturally led to logistical challenges—particularly in the equitable distribution of care. Consider the following questions.

1. What titles do you find mentioned in Acts 6:1-7?

2. Why were the seven selected? (See Acts 6:1-3)

3. Were the seven to be administrators or ministers? (See Acts 6:3.)

4. Were the seven to do all the ministry alone?

5. What action do you see in Acts 4:31-37 to meet the needs of others within the fellowship?

A shock about the early church for many of us is the absence of titles. The twelve disciples are called simply the Twelve. The seven men selected for ministry are not called deacons, elders or any other title, but are referred to simply as the Seven. Even as late as Paul's visit with Philip in Acts 21, Philip is referred to as an evangelist and as one of the seven: *Leaving the next day, we went on to Caesarea and stayed at the home of Philip the evangelist, who was one of the Seven. He had four unmarried daughters who prophesied* (Acts 21:8-9).

The only title mentioned in Acts 6:1-7 is that of brothers. This title is granted to the entire fellowship by grace. It cannot be earned. It points to a common ground upon which all believers stand.

The Seven were selected because of a problem that arose within the fellowship. The Greek-speaking Jewish believers felt that their widows were being neglected in the daily ministration of food and other provisions. The issue became so divisive that it threatened the fellowship of the church. The apostles realized that their role was a teaching/proclamation ministry. They knew that solving this problem was essential to the health and well-being of the church.

The apostles called the congregation together and charged them to select from within their ranks seven men who would be appointed over this ministry. The solution and ministry operation was up to these men. The emphasis in the selection of these seven was not upon a title to be conferred upon spiritual men. The emphasis was upon meeting the needs of widows who were being overlooked in ministry.

The Seven were appointed to be responsible over the ministry needed. Part of the debate concerning the ministry of deacons is whether they should be administrators or ministers. The New Testament pattern is that they are to be administrators of ministry. The Scripture states that the Seven were put over the ministry to the widows (Acts 6:3). They were responsible for seeing that the ministry was done—whether that meant doing the ministry themselves or enlisting others to help in the ministry.

When we remember that at least 5,000+ members were in the church or, as some believe, that as many as 25,000 by the time the dispute over ministry to the widows broke out, it is inconceivable that seven men could serve the needs of the fellowship. The evidence suggests that the Seven addressed the problem and oversaw the ministry to the widows by coordinating, motivating, and equipping others to serve.

We know that the entire church was in accord and assumed the responsibility of corporately meeting the needs of others. One particular man, Barnabas, is mentioned in meeting these needs and is not among the list of the seven found in Acts 6:1-7. It is consistent with the narrative to conclude the Seven coordinated the ministry already unfolding within the New Testament church.

A Model for Ministry

The experience of the early church in Acts 6 provides an excellent model for deacon ministry. Some critics raise the issue that the passage does not specifically refer to deacons and that it should not be used to frame deacon ministry. They suggest that men chosen by the congregation are simply called the Seven. They are not even called deacons.

A careful reading of the text reveals that the concept of deacons is found in Peter's words to the assembled church: *And the twelve summoned the full number of the disciples and said, "It is not right that we should give up preaching the word of God to **serve tables*** (Acts 6:2). Recall the definition of *diakonos*—a table waiter, a servant, a minister. When Peter spoke of serving tables, he interjected the concept of deacons into the early church. Granted, the idea was only seminal, but the selection of the Seven was the beginning of the diaconate. The dimensions of ministry revealed in this text provide useful insight into deacon ministry.

The Seven were chosen to meet a ministry need within the congregation. Peter gave the congregation requirements for these men. They had three qualifications: 1) a moral, 2) a spiritual, and 3) a gift qualification. The Seven had a moral qualification. They were to be men of honest report. The ministry with which they were dealing required that they be above reproach. They had a spiritual qualification. They were to be filled with the Holy Spirit. They had to be under the control of the Holy Spirit. They had a gift qualification. They were to have the gift of wisdom. This gift was needed to develop a solution for the situation the church was facing.

When these spiritual men of character exercised their spiritual gifts in ministry, the divisive problem was solved. The effect on the church was unity. Luke noted the result on the ministry of the early church: *And the word of God increased; and the number of the disciples multiplied in Jerusalem greatly; and a great company of priests were obedient to the faith* (Acts 6:7).

The concepts we find in the Acts 6 model offer some very constructive insights for deacon ministry. Deacon ministry should be filled by men who are morally qualified, filled with the Holy Spirit, and gifted for the specific ministry they are called to perform. When deacon ministry is effective, the church will be unified in fellowship and fruitful in evangelizing the lost.

The Purpose of Deacons in Your Church

Before we consider another way for deacons to serve, we might ask ourselves: What is the purpose of deacons, anyway? Are deacons leaders or servants, administrators or laborers, spiritual or social, necessary or optional? As you observe the work of deacons in your church, what is the present purpose of deacons in your church?

Notes and Observations

Session 3

The Role of the Holy Spirit
in Deacon Ministry

Jesus was in the upper room with His disciples celebrating Passo-
ver having what we call the last supper with them. The teachings
He gave His disciples on this evening before His arrest and cruci-
fixion form some of the more important teachings for believers of
His earthly ministry. He told the Twelve that He was going away
(Jn. 13:33). That statement prompted them to ask Jesus a series
of questions. In John 13:36, Peter asked, Where are you going?
In John 14:5, Thomas asked Him, If we don't know where you're
going, how can we know the way? Philip asked another question,
or, actually made a request of Jesus—Lord, shew us the Father,
and it will satisfy us (Jn. 14:8).

In response to Philip, Jesus stated that whoever had seen Him
had seen the Father. Jesus went on to say that the Father spoke
and worked through Him (v.10). He did not claim to do the
things He did on His own. Then He made the astounding statement (Jn. 14:12) that what He did, those who believe in Him shall
do and even greater things!

Seldom is John 14:12 ever addressed in most Christian circles. When it is, the tack taken to explain the meaning of the
verse concerns the scale of our institutional ministries such as
schools, hospitals, evangelistic and mission endeavors. It is difficult to get around the fact that Jesus said he that believeth on me
will do the things He did—even greater things. Jesus focused on
individual ministries not on institutional ministries. Interesting-
ly, Jesus followed His astounding statement with teachings about

the ministry of the Holy Spirit in believers' lives.

One of the more revealing passages about how Jesus lived His life and performed His ministry is Matthew 12:28. Jesus had been accused by the Pharisees of casting out demons by the power of Beelzebub (Mt. 12:24). Jesus said that He cast out demons by the Spirit of God. Jesus did not claim to have done the miraculous deeds in His own power, He stated that the means of the miracles was the Spirit. This is very instructive.

Jesus lived His life out of His humanity and not out of His divinity. Paul emphasized this to the Philippians when he wrote in 2:7 that Jesus made himself nothing (lit. *ekenosen*—to lay aside rank and privilege). Jesus, while fully human and fully divine, laid aside His rank and privilege to live His life as we do in order to provide a model for us. He lived His life in a way to show us how life was meant to be lived and how it could be lived.

The way Jesus lived—empowered by the Spirit and indwelt by the Father—is the way God wants all believers to live. Following His statement in John 14:12 that what He did we are to do and even greater things, Jesus said that the Holy Spirit would come to live within us (Jn. 14:16-17), that He (Jesus) would come to us (Jn. 14:18), that the Father and He would make their abode within us (Jn. 14:23). God—Father, Son, and Spirit—has come to live in us and to work His work through us! The ministry is God's, not ours. He simply wants to work through us as He worked through Jesus. He really is wanting our availability and not our ability. The key to us doing what Jesus did is our relationship to the Spirit, to Jesus, and to the Father. In our own power, we can do nothing (Jn. 15:5).

God has chosen to work through believers by giving each of them spiritual gifts and placing them in the church, the Body of

God's Method of Ministry

God's Power

God's power flows through the believer's life at the point of spiritual giftedness.

Faith
Giving
Helps

The Believer

For too long we have been trying to do God's work our way—using our strength, our resources, our intellect. **There is only one way to do God's work and that is to do it God's way!**

He has given to all believers spiritual gifts —grace gifts— that equip us for the ministries He has given us to do.

Christ, as it pleases Him to do the ministry that he has given each member to do (1 Cor. 12:18, 24-30). The gifts are the power point of God in our lives. They are the point at which His power flows through our lives to touch the world. Spiritual gifts are indicators of the ministry God wants a person to do. As deacons discover their gifts, they will be able to identify arenas of ministry to which God is calling them. This chapter and the next explore spiritual gifts and the role they play in equipping believers (including deacons) for ministry.

Gifted for Ministry

Now about spiritual gifts, brothers, I do not want you to be ignorant. You know that when you were pagans, somehow or other you were influenced and led astray to mute idols. Therefore I tell you that no one who is speaking by the Spirit of God says, "Jesus be cursed," and no one can say, "Jesus is Lord," except by the Holy Spirit.

— 1 Corinthians 12:1-3

In dealing with the problems of the Corinthian church, Paul deals with the issue of spiritual gifts—specifically the problems that the Corinthians were experiencing with this issue. He opened the section with a statement that he did not want the Corinthian Christians to be ignorant about spiritual gifts. The word Paul used in this text is an uncommon word—*pneumatikon*.

Pneumatikon refers to things emanating from the Holy Spirit, produced by the sole power of God Himself without natural instrumentality (Thayer). Most translators use the phrase, spiritual gifts, to interpret the meaning of Paul in 1 Corinthians 12:1. These gifts are spiritual in that they are given by the Holy Spirit (1 Cor. 12:7, 11) and are given to be used in our spiritual ministries. Paul wanted to be certain that the Corinthians had a clear and complete under-standing of their spiritual gifts, the special abilities equipping them for ministry that the Holy Spirit gives to all believers.

In most instances, when referring to the gifts of the Spirit, the writers of the New Testament used the words *charisma* (gift) or *charismata* (gifts). [See Rms. 12:6; 1 Cor. 7:7; 12:4, 9, 30, 31; 1 Peter 4:10.] The base of these words is *charis*—translated as grace—commonly understood as the unmerited favor of God. We generally talk about spiritual gifts when referring to gifts of the Spirit. A more accurate understanding or translation of *charisma* or *charismata* is grace gift or grace gifts.

Paul's opening statements affirm the common or universal role of the Holy Spirit in salvation (1 Cor. 12:2-3). Every believer comes to Christ drawn by the Holy Spirit. This salvation is a gift of grace and is foundational to all Christian experience. Paul immediately began a series of statements in his letter about the diversities of God's work in individual Christian lives. While no clear definition of a spiritual or grace gift is provided in the New

Testament, in his statements about God's various expressions and workings in Christians' lives, Paul provided us with an idea of what a spiritual gift is.

Now there are diversities of gifts, but the same Spirit. And there are differences of administrations, but the same Lord. And there are diversities of operations, but it is the same God which worketh all in all. But the manifestation of the Spirit is given to every man to profit withal.

— 1 Corinthians 12:4-7

What Is a Spiritual Gift?

In this passage, four different words are used by Paul that reveal insights into spiritual gifts. Paul used the words *gifts* (v. 4), *administrations* (v. 5), *operations* (v.6), and *manifestation* (v.7) in addressing the idea of spiritual gifts (1 Cor. 12:1). As a facetted diamond held up to the light glows with various colors as the light is diffracted, we see various dimensions to spiritual gifts as with each verse another facet is turned to the light. These words, taken as a composite, provide a sense of what is meant by spiritual gift.

Note these four words on the following chart—

Verse 4	χαρισμάτων	> *charismaton* = grace gifts
Verse 5	διακονίων	> *diakonion* = service/ministry
Verse 6	ένεργημάτων	> *energamaton* = empowerings/ workings
Verse 7	φανέρωσις	> *phanerosis* = revealing/ manifestation

33

In each verse, Paul used a different word referring to God's activity in the lives of believers. In 12:4, Paul used the word *charismaton*, a plural form translated as gifts. He emphasized the universality of the Spirit, but the diversity of gifts. In 12:5, he used the word *diakonion*, a word meaning ministries or services. He emphasized the diversity of ministries while pointing to the universality of the Lord. In 12:6, Paul stated the diversities of the workings, *energamaton*, while emphasizing the universality of God. In 12:7, Paul used a completely different word, *phanerosis*, meaning a revealing or a manifestation, in referring to the phenomenon of the Holy Spirit's work in our lives.

Read these verses—1 Corinthians 12:4-7. Look at the four words on the chart on the previous page. We can use these four words, to compose our own definition of a spiritual gift. (We don't have a convenient dictionary in the Bible...but we do have indicators.) Each descriptive word in these verses reveals a different facet of spiritual gifts. Combining them, we gain an understanding of what Paul meant by spiritual gift.

A spiritual gift is—a supernatural ability given by grace empowering believers for service and displaying the presence of God in our lives.

Key points come from Paul's comments in 1 Corinthians 12:4-11.

1. God gives spiritual gifts to different people according to His will.

2. How God has gifted us spiritually, determines the area of service—He expects us to perform.

3. When one does the particular service, called and equipped by God, an unusual energy for the work will be experienced.

4. When one performs the particular service God has called them to do, others will see the supernatural work of God through the servant.

Spiritual Gifts, Talents, and Skills

What's the difference between a spiritual gift, a natural talent, and a skill?

Aren't they all the same? The short answer is—no, they are not the same.

A spiritual gift is a supernatural evidence of God's presence in a Christian's life. The spiritual gift is given to equip and to empower us for the particular service or ministry that God has given us to do in and through the Body of Christ, the Church. Spiritual gifts come as a result of a spiritual birth. (It is unclear exactly when these gifts are given—at the salvation experience or as they are needed by the Church. God could do either. When is not nearly so important as the fact that they are given.)

A talent is a natural ability resulting from a natural birth. A talent is a result of the combination of the physical, psychological, emotional factors composing our natural bodies.

A skill is merely the learned application of spiritual gifts or natural talents.

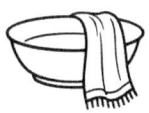 How would you explain the difference between a spiritual gift, a talent, and a skill?

You Have Charisma

God has gifted us for salvation. God in His grace has given us a variety of gifts. One of those gifts is salvation. The New Testament affirms that believers in Jesus Christ are saved by God's grace. Paul states this throughout his letters, but never more clearly than in his letter to the Ephesian Christians, For by grace are ye saved through faith; and that not of yourselves: it is the gift of God: not of works, lest any man should boast (Eph. 2:8-9). Salvation is an expression of God's grace—a free gift motivated by His love and mercy.

God has also gifted us for service. As believers, we have all been commissioned to ministry. God never commands us to do something without providing the necessary resources. Peter instructs us that every believer has been given a gift (or gifts) essential to the ministry that God has called us to do—As every man hath received the gift, even so minister the same to one another, as good stewards of the manifold grace of God (1 Peter 4:10).

A recent popular movement within the Christian community has so redefined the word and ideas behind *charismatic* that many Christians reject the word when applied to them. Rather than rejecting the concept of being charismatic, we need to define (or redefine in some instances) the concept. The term, *charismatic*, is merely a descriptor of a person who had been gifted by grace. All believers are charismatic because we have been gifted by God with saving grace and serving grace. Being charismatic is not just a perfectly good biblical concept, but one that is absolutely essential to our doing the ministry God has called us to do.

The grace gifts of God are essential to salvation and to service. The grace gifts are foundational to the very idea of being

Christian. Every believer has received God's gifts of grace—for salvation and for service—and is charismatic because of those gifts.

Why are the gifts given?

The New Testament presents three purposes of spiritual gifts.

 Read the following passages to see if you can identify those three purposes.

Purpose 1: 1 Corinthians 14:5,12,26; Ephesians 4:16

Purpose 2: 1 Peter 4:10

Purpose 3: 1 Peter 4:11

To build up the Church

The spiritual gifts are given to edify or build up the Body of Christ, the Church. The Church grows qualitatively and quantitatively—that is, spiritually and numerically. A church can grow in love, fellowship, obedience, ministry. In 1 Corinthians 14:5, 12, and 26, Paul repeats the constant theme—the Church is to receive edification, building up. Whatever the role of deacons in your church, they should be building up the Body of Christ.

This theme of edification or building up is repeated in Ephesians 4:16. In that passage, Paul uses the image of the body to emphasize that the Body—the Church—will be built up as each part performs its particular assignment.

The NIV states this clearly—*From Him the whole body, joined and held together by every supporting ligament, grows and builds itself up in love, as each part does its work* (Eph. 4:16). As we utilize our gifts in ministry, new believers will be brought to faith in Christ. As other believers teach and minister, the new believers will be developed or matured in their faith. The net effect is the Church will be built up.

To minister to one another

The Apostle Peter in his first epistle addressed the concept of spiritual gifts. In many ways, the letter is a "primer" for Christian living—addressing the basic issues of Christian living. In 1 Peter 4:10, Peter writes—As every man hath received the gift, even so minister the same one to another, as good stewards of the manifold grace of God.

The word Peter used for gift was charisma. He states that every believer has received a grace gift to be used in ministry to one another. Spiritual gifts equip believers (all believers—including deacons) for ministry. The ministry is both within and without the Body. In his statement, Peter focuses upon the ministry to one another. Dr. Findley Edge writes in *The Doctrine of the Laity*—

If you are a Christian, you are gifted. The spiritual gift was not given to you primarily for your benefit or primarily for your enjoyment. Paul said the gifts are given for profiting (1 Cor. 12:7). Peter said the gifts are given to minister to each other (1 Pt. 4:10). Gifts are for the common good and ultimately for fulfilling God's purpose in the world.

To glorify God

The theme of gifts continues in 1 Peter 4:11 where we are provided some guidelines for using gifts—*If any person speak, let him speak as the oracles of God; if any man minister, let him do it as of the ability which God giveth: that God in all things may be glorified through Jesus Christ, to whom be praise and dominion for ever and ever. Amen.*

How does this verse compare to our definition of spiritual gifts?

Remember it—***a gift is a supernatural ability given by grace empowering believers for service and displaying the presence of God in our lives.***

What does Peter state as a purpose of grace gifts in this verse?

To glorify God—what does it mean? The word Peter used that is translated glorified means to make renowned, render illustrious, that is, to cause the dignity and worth of some person or thing to become manifest and acknowledged (Thayer p.157). When a Christian uses his or her gift in ministry, God's worth and person are manifested to those who see the gift exercised or who are the recipients of the benefits of the gift. Jesus referred to this in the Sermon on the Mount—*Let your light so shine before men, that they may see your good works, and glorify your Father which is in heaven* (Mt. 5:16).

The basic meaning behind the word, glory, is a brightness, an effulgence, radiance, a shining forth. When we bring glory to God two things occur. First, He shines through our lives—we reflect His radiance. Second, when our lives reflect the light of God, the world sees God—we "shed light" on God so those around us can see Him.

Through the exercise of our gifts, the world receives the reflection of God's light and God is seen more clearly.

Purpose of Gifts

To continue the work of Christ...Jn. 14:12

He founded the Church...Mt. 16:18

We are to build up the Church...1 Cor. 14:5,12,26

He came as a servant...Mk. 10:45

We are to serve one another...1 Pt. 4:10

He glorified the Father...Jn. 17:1-4

We are to glorify God...1 Pt. 4:11

Spiritual gifts are given to Christians who become deacons for the same reasons. Deacons are to build up the Body of Christ, to minister to the needs of others, and to glorify God. The specific service will be determined by the particular gifts given to each deacon individually and to the deacon group as a whole.

What Are the New Testament Gifts?

Several New Testament passages deal with spiritual gifts. The primary passages are found in the writings of Paul and Peter. Both men provide great insight into the operation of spiritual gifts in the lives of individual believers and in the life of the Church. Paul provides us with several lists of spiritual gifts.

In discussions today much is made of various lists of gifts. Different persons emphasize different lists depending upon their theological orientations. Some focus primarily on the list of gifts in the Corinthian letter—mostly because of the prominence of the gifts of tongues, healing and miracles. Others find the list found in Romans to be more acceptable—probably because tongues, healing, and miracles are not mentioned. Some current writers use a list of nine gifts, others fourteen, others fifteen or sixteen. One recent study went to the other extreme and provided no list whatever—confusing the issue even more.

Some don't care for any list because they believe gifts are no longer operable. They interpret Paul's statement in 1 Corinthians 13:8-10 to invalidate gifts. Paul states that prophecy, tongues, knowledge will cease (v.8). At some point, the partial will give way when the perfect is come (v.10). They interpret *perfect* to refer to the Scripture (i.e.—when the Bible was completed, the gifts were invalidated).

This proof-texting fails to consider Paul's further comment— *Now we see but a poor reflection as in a mirror; then we shall see face to face. Now I know in part; then I shall know fully, even as I am fully known* (v.12). The validity of gifts is a now and then issue. ***Now*** obviously refers to the present; ***then*** refers to a future point. When ***then*** comes, we will see face to face and know as we are known. Obviously, this means when we see the Lord face to face (because of death or because Christ returns). At that point, we will no longer know in part, but we will know fully as we are fully known. At that point, gifts no longer will be needed.

Until then, the gifts, all the gifts, are valid.

The best list to use is the list in the New Testament. Many people and churches have long accepted the Bible as our authority in matters of faith and practice. Since the Bible is authoritative, the New Testament list is adequate and acceptable.

What are the gifts in the New Testament? Look at the following key passages from Paul's writings. You might want to make a chart by looking at the various passages and listing under each the specific gifts you discover in each passage.

- Romans 12:6-8

- 1 Corinthians 7:7, 12:8-10, 28-30

- Ephesians 4:11

This will be a good exercise for you. And when you are done, compare your list with the chart found on page 54. A few notes in the box on page 53 might be helpful to your understanding.

The Church—The Body of Christ

Many images are used in the New Testament to help us understand the Church. It is compared to an army, a bride, a building, a flock, leaven, fire, branches, a family. Of all these, the imagery of the human body is the most widely used. Paul used this extensively in Romans, 1 Corinthians, Ephesians and Colossians. The image of the body helps us understand several aspects of the Church and the ministry of deacons.

The Structure of the Body

Christ is the Head; we are the Body (Col. 1:18). As Head of the

Body, He controls the actions of His Body. He is Lord of life, directing the various members of the Body as they perform His will. Jesus controls and directs the work of the Church. In our physical bodies, when we lift an arm, the muscles are merely responding to the impulses of the brain directing the muscles to contract. Similarly, Jesus controls the actions of the members of His Body, the Church.

Whatever the role deacons are perceived to perform, that role must accept Christ as the Head—controlling and directing this part of Christ's Body.

The Function of the Body

God has given each member of the human body a place in the body and a function to perform. He has done the same with the spiritual Body of Christ (1 Cor.12: 18-30). Paul called the Corinthians the Body of Christ and members in particular (1 Corinthians 12:27). God has given each member of the Body a function to perform. He equips the members of the Body with spiritual gifts. These spiritual gifts enable us to perform the tasks God has given. Several basic facts help us understand how God intends the Church to function.

1. All members have gifts. First Corinthians 12:7 and 11 emphasize that every person in the Body has a gift or gifts. We are all charismatic—grace gifted. We have been gifted by God for salvation and service. God never asks us to do a task without giving us the necessary resources to do that task.

2. All members do not have the same gifts. Romans 12:6 reveals that we differ in our gifts by God's design and grace. The Church is a well designed organism. Homogeneity is fine in milk, but terrible in the Church. Can you imagine how gross the body would be if it were all one part? Speaking of our differences, Dr. Findley Edge has said, "We must learn to celebrate our differences, not merely to tolerate them." Praise God for the differences!

3. <u>All members are placed in the Body by God</u>. God controls the Church. At any given time and place, we are where we are by the will of God. We are gifted to serve in particular situations. God supplies members of the Body with the gifts they need to serve Him. God also supplies each expression of the Body with those gifted members it needs. This assures each local church that it has the essential resources to do the ministry God has for it.

4. <u>All members are necessary for the Body to function as it should</u>. Paul emphasized to the Ephesian Christians the necessity of each part of the Body. The New International Version makes Paul's emphasis clear—From him the whole body, joined and held together by every supporting ligament, grows and builds itself up in love, as each part does its work (Ephesians 4:16). As each member contributes his or her ministry to the whole, the Church will grow and be built up. To the degree that each member does not contribute to the whole, the Church to that extent will fail to grow or to be built up.

These distinctions are in deacons as well as in the membership as a whole. The diversity of gifts within a deacon group will reflect the diversity necessary for the ministry they are to perform.

The Rainbow

Another image that has something significant to teach us about spiritual gifts is the image of a rainbow.

How many colors in a rainbow?   2   3   4   5   6

Actually a rainbow has three colors—red, yellow, and blue—the three primary colors. The six colors that make up the rainbows that we see in the sky are composed from those three primary colors. Red and yellow combine to make orange; yellow and blue combine to make green; and blue and red combine to make violet. (And yes, we do know that an actual rainbow is made by a refraction of light into its different wave lengths and we know about white, black, infrared, and ultraviolet—just a note to those of you who like to complicate a nice, simple, little illustration!)

The point that relates to spiritual gifts is that just as three primary colors combine to make the other colors of a "rainbow," the unique combination of gifts that an individual possesses combines to create a unique ministry that contributes to the work of the Church and the kingdom. The unique combination of spiritual gifts in the deacons of your church, reflect the unique ministry God expects from your particular deacon ministry. To copy what another church is doing without regard to the spiritual giftedness of your deacons is to ignore God's special equipping for your specific ministry.

The three, four or five gifts that surface as strongest in your life, "color" your rainbow—your giftedness. Within the range of these primary gifts you will find your special contribution and ministry. Within the range of the gifts possessed by your deacon group as a whole will be the special ministry your deacon group is to perform.

The Multiplication of Ministry
Gifts/Body/Synergism

The combination of an individual's gifts equips him to make a unique contribution to kingdom ministry. The various gifts a person possesses sets up within that person a synergy. ***Synergy is*** *the cooperative action of individual agencies such that the total effect is greater than the two effects taken independently.*

Well...that's what it is!

Now this is what it means—the total is greater than the sum of the parts. Synergy has a multiplying effect. In synergy 1+1=3. The rainbow that has only three basic colors but looks like it has six illustrates synergy. Synergy has a multiplying effect.

A person's combination of gifts has a greater effect than any one gift taken by itself. For instance, the gift of teaching combined with the gifts of knowledge and leadership prepares a person to be a more effective teacher. The ability to teach provides an effective avenue for using knowledge. The gift of leadership allows a platform for exercising the other two gifts.

This same effect is found in the Body as a whole. The individual members of the Body have a multiplying impact in ministry. Our individual ministries are complimentary to one another and contribute to the mission Christ has given us. When each part of the Body is functioning with the gifts God has given, a powerful effect is created. Paul noted this effect in his Ephesian letter—*From him the whole body, joined and held together by every supporting ligament, grows and builds itself up in love, as each part does its work* (4:16). The effect of each part doing its work is that the Body grows and builds itself up in love.

We are interdependent, not independent. We must see our lives in relation to the other members of the Body. No individual has all the gifts necessary to perform the function of the whole. In the Body, interdependence creates a greater strength. The Old Testament states that where one can rout a thousand, two can rout ten-thousand (Dt. 32:30). The two relying on one another and God increase their strength. Another image that shows strength from reliance is the image of a rope—*a cord of three strands is not quickly broken* (Ecc. 4:12). Where a single strand has a certain strength, when braided with additional strands, its strength is greater than the sum of the individual strands. Its strength is actually multiplied. This is synergism.

When we see ourselves as independent—as separate from one another—we set ourselves up for difficulties within the Body. Like a cancer within the Body, we become centered upon ourselves, our needs, our wants, our desires—even our gifts and our ministries.

Spiritual giftedness for ministry not only allows for, but encourages differences. The greater the differences, the greater the strength. Plywood has great strength because of the different-grained wood layers running in different directions. Each layer is very thin. By itself a layer is relatively weak. When glued with the grain of other layers running in all those different directions, its strength is multiplied.

Differences are built into the Church by God. Just as He designed differences into the human body, He designed differences into the Body of Christ, the Church. The Church was never intended to be a homogeneous body. Remember Paul's question to the Corinthians—*If the whole were an eye, where were the hearing?* Homogenized milk is probably a good thing—but a homogenized church isn't. Our strength comes from our differences.

Within the combination of our individual grace gifts is the ministry that God has given each person to do. Within the differences built into the church is the ministry that God has given each church to do. When we each discover God's gifts in our individual lives and in the church as a whole, we find indicators or clues to the ministries God has given us to do.

The image of the Church as a Body found in much of Paul's writings illustrates a better way of "doing church." This image helps us understand that all members of the Church have individual places of responsibility in the life and work of the Church just as members of the physical body have their places.

God has already designed the Church. He has put the Church together in such a way as to perform the mission He has for it to accomplish. *But now hath God set the members every one of them in the body, as it hath pleased him....but God hath tempered the body together, having given more abundant honour to that part which lacked: That there should be no schism in the body; but that the members should have the same care for one another* (1 Cor. 12:18,24,25).

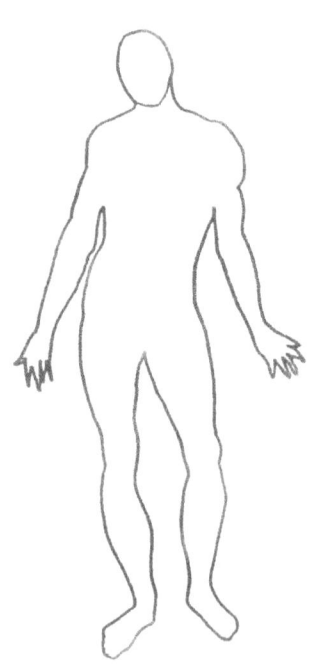

Rivers of Living Water

Jesus said that the presence of the Holy Spirit would be a source of living water. *He that believeth on me, as the scripture hath said, out of his belly shall flow rivers of living water. (But this spake he of the Spirit, which they that believe on him should receive: for the Holy Ghost was not yet given; because that Jesus was not yet glorified.)* —John 7:38-39

Living water is an image of contrast with water from a well. When water is drawn from a well, it takes work to get it out of the ground and work to get it to where it is needed. In contrast, the spring flows effortlessly to the surface with cool, fresh water.

In the panhandle of Florida is Emerald Springs, a large spring system. Most of this system is gently bubbling up through the sandy bottom or filtering through porous, honey-comb limestone. This area is beautifully placid, but one part of the spring system rushes out of a deep gash in the ground, large enough to swallow a car. A million gallons a day gushes from the spring. The force of the current is so great that swimmers cannot make headway against it. Getting into the mouth of the spring requires holding to rocks to keep from being swept away. Standing in the mouth of the spring, one feels the force of an endless supply of cool, clear, life-giving water.

The Holy Spirit's presence in our lives produces a powerful, never-ending river of living water. When we are serving out of our giftedness, the Spirit flows through us—energizing our lives and ministries with power and joy. The difference in a Spirit-empowered ministry and one driven by our own intellect and resources is the difference between a rushing spring of water and water drawn from a well.

God has chosen to work through believers by the spiritual gifts He gives. Spiritual gifts are the ***modus operandi*** of ministry. Search the Scriptures. No where are we told to just go do the best we can in our own power. Quite the opposite. At the Ascension, Jesus told the disciples to wait for the empowerment of the Spirit before they did anything (Acts 1:4). Only after they were empowered by the Spirit were they to be His witnesses (Acts 1:8).

The power of God intersects the church and the world at the point of our spiritual gifts. When we discover our gifts and begin serving out of them the power of God flows through us to touch others and change lives.

Notes and Observations

Notes and Observations

Notes on the following composite list of grace gifts from the Apostle Paul:

- Prophecy and teaching in all three lists can imply the importance of these two gifts to the church.

- Each list is different. No list is definitive.

- The gifts listed might only represent the broader spectrum of spiritual gifts. [God is not bound, He could give to the church any special abilities He chooses—but at least we have these lists through revelation.] Paul did not know the Roman church, the gifts are broad and general in nature. The list of "gifts" in Ephesians is not exactly a list of gifts, it is actually a list of *gifted persons*—leaders in the church. The list implies gifts the leaders would possess—a prophet would have the gift of prophecy; an evangelist would possess the gift of evangelism. The length of the Corinthian list could reflect the difficulty the Corinthian church had with the issue of gifts.

The lists use very specific words for the gifts. Celibacy is implied.			
Gift		Transliteration	Text
Prophecy/Prophet	προφητειαν	propheteian	Rm. 12:6, 1 Cor. 12:29 Eph. 4:11
Ministry/Service	διακονία	diakonia	Rm. 12:7
Teaching	διδάσκαλιά	didaskalia	Rm. 12:7 1 Cor. 12:29 Eph. 4:11
Encouragement	παρακλησίς	paraklesis	Rm. 12:8
Giving	μέταδιδους	metadidous	Rm. 12:8
Administration	προϊστάμενος	proistamenos	Rm. 12:8
Mercy	έλεων	eleon	Rm. 12:8
Celibacy	(derived from the context)		1 Cor. 7:7
Wisdom	σοφίας	sophias	1 Cor. 12:8
Knowledge	γνώσεως	gnoseos	1 Cor. 12:9
Faith	πίστις	pistis	1 Cor. 12:9
Healings	ίαμάτων	iamaton	1 Cor. 12:9 1 Cor. 12:28
Miracles	δυνάμεων	dunameon	1 Cor. 12:10 1 Cor. 12:28
Discernment	διακρίσεις	diakriseis	1 Cor. 12:10
Tongues	γλωσσων	glosson	1 Cor 12:10 1 Cor. 12:28
Interpretation	έρμηνεία	diermeneia	1 Cor. 12:10
Apostleship/Apostle	απόστολοι	apostoloi	1 Cor. 12:29 Eph. 4:11
Helps	αντιλήψεις	antilepseis	1 Cor. 12:28
Evangelism/Evangelist	εύαγγελιστάς	euaggelistas	Eph. 4:11
Shepherding/Pastor	ποιμέας	poimenas	Eph. 4:11
Governments	κυβερνήσεις	kuberneseis	1 Cor. 12:28

Session 4

The Role of the Holy Spirit
in Your Ministry

Spiritual gifts are given to equip believers for the ministry God
has called each of us to perform. The gifts are not just for us to
admire or show off. If we do not use the gifts in ministry, we
frustrate the very purposes of God. To be more effective stewards
of the grace God has entrusted to us, we need to discover, develop, and deploy our gifts in ministry.

Discovering Our Gifts

Gifts can be discovered in several ways.

1. Inventories

Several inventories are available to aid in the discovery of spiritual gifts. The one in this manual (used by permission) was developed by the Adult Section of the Discipleship Training Department of the Baptist Sunday School Board (now LifeWay). Over
a period of three years, thousands of participants helped validate
this inventory to a 90 percentile range of accuracy. (And know,
at best, inventories are indicators.) The inventory is a series of
statements requiring a response. Point values are assigned by the
participant to each statement. The statements have been developed around the spiritual gifts listed in the New Testament. Participants' responses to the statements indicate areas of giftedness.

2. Identification by others

Other members of the church have an objective view of our ministry. Sometimes they may see a gift at work through our lives.

The story of George Truett's call to the ministry is a prime illustration of others seeing one's ministry and identifying it. It was a deacon in a Saturday church conference who suggested that young George Truett be ordained to the gospel ministry. George then struggled with the decision for the balance of the day and evening, finally surrendering to the will of God and the church.

This man was called to pastor a church—to enter full time vocational Christian service—by a church that wanted him to be their pastor. He had no particular persuasion of a call from God until after the deacon proposed his ordination. He heeded the call, became a pastor, and ultimately left a stellar record as a preacher of the gospel and as pastor of First Baptist Church of Dallas, Texas—a church he pastored for forty-seven years.

An interesting activity (probably best done in groups that know one another fairly well) is to allow a time of sharing in which group members identify the gifts of others. Often, individuals are totally unaware that they are displaying any particular gift. They are just doing what comes naturally—or better yet, supernaturally.

3. In-service Experience

Persons can identify their gifts by taking on a variety of tasks in and through the church. Ministry in an area related to your spiritual gift will be easy and enjoyable. Jesus said the Holy Spirit would produce from within us rivers of living water (John 7:38-39). Ministry related to your giftedness will flow from you. God's power flows through our lives to touch the world in ministry at the point of our spiritual gifts.

If we serve outside of our gifts, we operate in our own strength and not in God's. Jesus told the disciples they would be His witnesses (Acts 1:4-8). The sequence of His words is significant—*But ye shall receive power after that the Holy Ghost is come upon you: and ye shall be witnesses unto me...*(v.8). The disciples were to be witnesses but only after the Holy Spirit had come upon them. Jesus was even more specific in the version given in Luke's gospel—*And, behold, I send the promise of my Father upon you: but tarry ye in the city of Jerusalem, until ye be endued with power from on high* (Lk. 24:49).

The power for ministry is linked directly to the Holy Spirit's presence in believers' lives. Had the disciples tried to witness without the power of the Spirit, they would have been serving in their own strength—and nothing would have come of it. Jesus had told them earlier...*without me ye can do nothing* (Jn. 15:5). The ministry is not ours; the power is not ours—they are both God's. If you struggle and strain to do a task, if it leaves you drained and down, odds are you are serving outside your gift. Experimenting with a variety of tasks can help identify your gifts. Where you feel the empowerment of God is probably where you are gifted.

Developing Our Gifts

Paul urged Timothy to *neglect not the gift that is in thee* (1Tim. 4:14) and to *stir up the gift of God* (2 Tim. 1:6). Once we discover our gifts, we should give ourselves to developing them. But, let's understand what we mean by developing our gifts. A reasonable question to ask is, Can gifts be developed? After all, God gives us these gifts of grace. Are we trying to improve on His handiwork?

Not to put too fine a point on the subject, we are probably not talking of developing the gifts so much as we are developing our knowledge of the gifts, learning how and with whom they can be used, and developing the skills necessary to utilize the gifts to their fullest potential. For instance, a person might have the gift of teaching. While the person might be a gifted communicator because of the gift of teaching, skills in using teaching aids, techniques, and methods or understanding the psychology and process of learning can be developed to make the gift of teaching much more effective.

Development of gifts is done by three primary means.

1. Education

Gifts can be developed or sharpened through study. In the verses immediately following the one where Paul urged Timothy not to neglect his gift, he instructed Timothy to meditate and to give attention to doctrine or teaching (1 Tim. 4:15-16). Study gives us a knowledge base from which we can work. Our study can acquaint us with facts about our gifts that can make us more effective in using our gifts in ministry.

2. Exercise

Another means of developing gifts is simply to use your gift in some kind of service. The old adage that experience is the best teacher applies here. At times it appears that we study and study and study—never applying the teachings we learn to life and labor. We keep gathering facts and knowledge, but never using them. It is similar to a body builder who studies physiology, anatomy, and nutrition continuously, but never lifts any weights. He knows all about the subject of body building, but he's not doing anything with the knowledge.

The most effective pattern of development might be to discover the gift, assign the person to a ministry, and then offer some type of training or education. The need for the education would be far more evident if the gift was being exercised in some kind of service.

3. Example

Example is one of the most powerful means available to those trying to develop the gifts of others. For instance, consider how parental examples are indelibly imprinted on the fabric of children. Traits, language, habits surface in the life of a growing child that can be traced to a parent's example.

Jesus recognized the power of example. He taught by example. Stressing the importance of service to one another, Jesus washed His disciples' feet at the last supper. When seated with them again, He said, *I've given you an example that you should do as I have done to you* (John 13:15).

Paul urged Timothy to be an example of the believers in his words, life-style, love, spirit, faith, and purity of life (1 Tim. 4:12). Paul knew a good example was the best teaching model and personal witness for others.

A good means of developing a gift is to follow the example of another believer who possesses and uses that same gift in an effective manner. In trades of all types, apprenticeship is a valued means of developing skills and craftsmanship. An apprenticeship program in our churches could be an effective means of developing spiritual gifts.

Deploying Our Gifts

If spiritual gifts are never deployed in service, any study of gifts becomes merely a mental exercise in futility. Gifts have been given to use. If allowed to lie fallow, gifts fail to fulfill their God-given function. We have a stewardship of grace—*As every man hath received the gift, even so minister the same one to another, as good stewards of the manifold grace of God* (1 Peter 4:10). As stewards, we will give an account to our Master for the way we have used or abused the resources He has placed in our care. One day God will require us to account for what we have done with the entrustments He has given to us. Spiritual gifts have been given to us for use in ministry to one another. Within this purpose is the basis for our accountability.

Two arenas exist in which gifts should be deployed—one is the church, the other is the world.

1. The Church

The church offers opportunities to utilize a wide range of gifts. Ministry within the structure of the church family calls for a variety of persons and gifts. A variety of needs engage believers in ministry to one another. The program organizations (Sunday school, discipleship, missions, music) require people to serve as teachers, leaders, directors. Committees give outlets for many believers to serve the church with their gifts. Worship services and outreach efforts engage other members' gifts. Ministries of support, care, and equipping within the church family provide occasions to express our love for one another.

2. The World

Ministry, however, should not stop with our own. If it does, we will fail to use all the gifts God has given us. Dr. Findley Edge has long promoted the concept of "lay" ministry. He observes that only 20% of a church's membership is required to maintain the organizations of the church and conduct the ministry "within the walls of the church." The other 80% will find their arena of ministry in the world.

Every believer has his or her own "world." It is the sphere within which they operate. It includes their families, neighborhoods, circles of friends, business acquaintances. The great Quaker theologian, Dr. Elton Trueblood, has written that the vast majority of church members will find their ministry outside the church walls as ministers of common life. In this arena, the great majority of the church membership will find their ministries in their families, communities, vocations, or in specific ministry/ mission projects.

The Inventory

Following is an inventory that will help you identify the gifts the Holy Spirit has given to equip you for your ministry. Taking the inventory requires about an hour.

Before you begin—just a few comments...

This is not a test, so there are no wrong answers. The inventory consists of 103 items. Some of these reflect concrete actions; others are descriptive traits; and still others are statements of belief. You are asked to indicate how descriptive each item is of you.

Record your response by placing in the blank beside each item the number which corresponds to the answer you want. Your response choices are:

5 - Highly characteristic of me/definitely true for me.

4 - Most of the time this would describe me/be true for me.

3 - Frequently characteristic of me/true for me—about 50% of the time.

2 - Occasionally characteristic of me—about 25% of the time.

1 - Not at all characteristic of me/definitely untrue for me.

Do not spend too much time on any one item. Remember, it is not a test. Mark the extent to which you feel the item is descriptive of you. Usually your immediate response is best.

Please give a response for each item. Do not skip any items.

Do not ask others how they are answering or how they think you should answer. Work at your own pace.

Spiritual Gifts Inventory

_____ 1. I have the ability to organize ideas, resources, time, and people effectively.

_____ 2. I am willing to study and prepare for the task of teaching.

_____ 3. I am able to relate the truths of God to specific situations.

_____ 4. I inspire persons to right actions by pointing out the blessings of this path.

_____ 5. I have a God-given ability to help others grow in their faith.

_____ 6. I possess a special ability to communicate the truth of salvation.

_____ 7. I am sensitive to the hurts of people.

_____ 8. I experience joy in meeting needs through sharing possessions.

_____ 9. I enjoy study.

_____ 10. I have delivered God's messages of warning and judgment.

_____ 11. I am able to sense the true motivations of persons and movements.

_____ 12. I trust God in difficult situations.

_____ 13. I have a strong desire to contribute to the establishment of new churches.

_____ 14. I feel God has used me in a supernatural event.

_____ 15. I enjoy doing things for people in need.

_____ 16. I am aware of a special appropriation of God's healing power through myself.

_____ 17. I have been moved to express such intense spiritual feelings that what came from my mouth was unintelligible to most people.

_____ 18. Words or thoughts come to me in an inspiring way after a message in an unknown language is delivered in group worship.

_____ 19. I can delegate and assign meaningful work.

_____ 20. I have an ability and desire to teach.

_____ 21. I am usually able to analyze a situation correctly.

_____ 22. I have a tendency to encourage and reward others.

_____ 23. I am willing to take the initiative in helping other Christians grow in their faith.

_____ 24. I am unafraid to share with lost people.

_____ 25. I have an acute awareness of such emotions as loneliness, pain, fear, and anger in others.

_____ 26. I am a cheerful giver.

_____ 27. I spend time digging into facts.

_____ 28. I feel that I have a message from God to deliver to others.

_____ 29. I can recognize when a person is genuine/honest.

_____ 30. I am willing to yield to God's will rather than question and waver.

_____ 31. I would like to be more active in getting the gospel to people in other lands.

_____ 32. I have been used by God to bring about supernatural changes.

_____ 33. It makes me happy to do things for people in need.

_____ 34. I am willing to be an instrument of healing.

_____ 35. I have had an awareness of wanting to praise God in utterances which one's heart feels but which one's mind does not understand.

_____ 36. I have prayed that I may interpret if someone begins speaking in tongues.

_____ 37. I am successful in getting a group to do its work joyfully.

_____ 38. I have the ability to plan learning approaches.

_____ 39. I have been able to offer solutions to spiritual problems others are facing.

_____ 40. I can identify those who need encouragement.

_____ 41. I have trained Christians to be more obedient disciples of Christ.

_____ 42. I am willing to do whatever it takes to see others come to Christ.

_____ 43. I am attracted to people who are hurting.

_____ 44. I am a generous giver.

_____ 45. I am able to discover new truths.

_____ 46. I have spiritual insights from Scripture concerning issues and people which compel me to speak out.

_____ 47. I can sense when a person is acting in accord with God's will.

_____ 48. I can trust God even when things look dark.

_____ 49. I have a strong desire to take the gospel to places where it has never been heard.

_____ 50. I have been used by God to accomplish a miracle.

_____ 51. I enjoy helping people.

_____ 52. I understand scriptural teachings regarding healing.

_____ 53. I believe that speaking in tongues may be edifying to the Lord's Body.

_____ 54. I am able to interpret the ecstatic utterances of others.

_____ 55. I have been able to make effective and efficient plans for accomplishing the goals of a group.

_____ 56. I understand the variety of ways people learn.

_____ 57. I am often consulted when fellow Christians are struggling to make difficult decisions.

_____ 58. I think about how I can comfort and encourage others in my congregation.

_____ 59. I am able to give spiritual direction to others.

_____ 60. I am able to present the gospel to lost persons in such a way that they accept the Lord and His salvation.

_____ 61. I possess an unusual capacity to understand the feelings of those in distress.

_____ 62. I have a strong sense of stewardship based on the recognition of God's ownership of all things.

_____ 63. I know where to get information.

_____ 64. I have delivered to other persons messages which have come directly from God.

_____ 65. I can sense when a person is acting under God's leadership.

_____ 66. I try to be continually in God's will.

_____ 67. I feel I should take the gospel to people who have different beliefs from me.

_____ 68. I have been God's instrument to bring about supernatural change in lives or events.

_____ 69. I love to do things for people.

_____ 70. I am aware of the miraculous aspects of life.

_____ 71. I enjoy being with persons who speak in tongues.

_____ 72. I have prayed that I may be able to interpret tongues.

_____ 73. I am skilled in setting forth positive and precise steps of action.

_____ 74. I explain Scripture in such a way that others understand it.

_____ 75. I can usually see spiritual solutions to problems.

_____ 76. I am glad when people who need comfort, consolation, encouragement, and counsel seek my help.

_____ 77. I am able to nurture others.

_____ 78. I feel at ease in sharing Christ with nonbelievers.

_____ 79. I recognize the signs of stress and distress in others.

_____ 80. I desire to give generously and unpretentiously to worthwhile projects and ministries.

_____ 81. I can organize facts into meaningful relationships.

_____ 82. God gives me messages to deliver to His people.

_____ 83. I am able to sense whether people are being honest when they tell of their religious experiences.

_____ 84. I try to be available for God to use.

_____ 85. I enjoy presenting the gospel to persons of other cultures and backgrounds.

_____ 86. I have been used by God to bring about a powerful act which could not be explained in human terms.

_____ 87. I enjoy doing little things that help people.

_____ 88. I am aware of the supernatural power at work within my life.

_____ 89. Speaking in tongues enables me to be more effective in all areas of my life.

_____ 90. I can plan a strategy and "bring others aboard."

_____ 91. I can give a clear, uncomplicated presentation.

_____ 92. I have been able to apply biblical truth to the specific needs of my church.

_____ 93. God has used me to encourage others to live Christ-like lives.

_____ 94. I have sensed the need to help other people become more effective in their ministries.

_____ 95. I like to talk about Jesus to those who do not know Him.

_____ 96. I feel assured that a situation will change for the glory of God even when the situation seems impossible.

_____ 97. I am able to nurture others.

_____ 98. I have an awareness that God still heals people as He did in biblical times.

_____ 99. I have matured in my spiritual life as a result of speaking in tongues.

_____100. I sense God's intervention in events.

_____101. I have witnessed miraculous answers to my prayers.

_____102. I believe God can and does act in miraculous ways.

_____103. I have a burning desire to see people who are suffering be made well.

Now...score yourself.

On the next page you will find the scoring instrument. Follow these instructions:

1. For each gift place in the boxes the number of the response you gave for each item indicated below the box.

2. For each gift add the numbers in the boxes and put the total (sum) in the "TOTAL" box.

3. For each gift divide the TOTAL by the number indicated and place the result in the "SCORE" box (round each answer to one decimal place, such as 3.7). This is your score for the gift.

Gift   (Hint: score more quickly, fill the boxes vertically)

Leadership   ☐ + ☐ + ☐ + ☐ + ☐ +
Item 1   Item 19   Item 37   Item 55   Item 73

☐ = ☐ ÷ 6 = ☐
Item 90   TOTAL   **SCORE**

Teaching   ☐ + ☐ + ☐ + ☐ + ☐ +
Item 2   Item 20   Item 38   Item 56   Item 74

☐ = ☐ ÷ 6 = ☐
Item 91   TOTAL   **SCORE**

Knowledge   ☐ + ☐ + ☐ + ☐ + ☐ +
Item 9   Item 27   Item 45   Item 63   Item 81

☐ = ☐ ÷ 6 = ☐
Item 96   TOTAL   **SCORE**

Wisdom   ☐ + ☐ + ☐ + ☐ + ☐ +
Item 3   Item 21   Item 39   Item 57   Item 75

☐ = ☐ ÷ 6 = ☐
Item 92   TOTAL   **SCORE**

Prophecy   ☐ + ☐ + ☐ + ☐ + ☐ =
Item 10   Item 28   Item 46   Item 64   Item 82

☐ ÷ 5 = ☐
TOTAL   **SCORE**

Spiritual
Discernment   ☐ + ☐ + ☐ + ☐ + ☐ =
Item 11   Item 29   Item 47   Item 65   Item 83

☐ ÷ 5 = ☐
TOTAL   **SCORE**

Encouragement   ☐ + ☐ + ☐ + ☐ + ☐ +
Item 4   Item 22   Item 40   Item 58   Item 76

☐ = ☐ ÷ 6 = ☐
Item 93   TOTAL   **SCORE**

66

Shepherding

□ + □ + □ + □ + □ +
Item 5   Item 23   Item 41   Item 59   Item 77

□ = □ ÷ 6 = □
Item 94   TOTAL   **SCORE**

Faith

□ + □ + □ + □ + □ +
Item 12   Item 30   Item 48   Item 66   Item 84

□ = □ ÷ 6 = □
Item 97   TOTAL   **SCORE**

Evangelism

□ + □ + □ + □ + □ +
Item 6   Item 24   Item 42   Item 60   Item 78

□ = □ ÷ 6 = □
Item 95   TOTAL   **SCORE**

Apostleship

□ + □ + □ + □ + □ =
Item 13   Item 31   Item 49   Item 67   Item 85

□ ÷ 5 = □
TOTAL   **SCORE**

Miracles

□ + □ + □ + □ + □ =
Item 14   Item 32   Item 50   Item 68   Item 86

□ ÷ 5 = □
TOTAL   **SCORE**

Helps

□ + □ + □ + □ + □ =
Item 15   Item 33   Item 51   Item 69   Item 87

□ ÷ 5 = □
TOTAL   **SCORE**

Mercy

□ + □ + □ + □ + □ =
Item 7   Item 25   Item 43   Item 61   Item 79

□ ÷ 5 = □
TOTAL   **SCORE**

67

Giving

[　　] + [　　] + [　　] + [　　] + [　　] =
Item 8　　Item 26　　Item 44　　Item 62　　Item 80

[　　] ÷ 5 = [　　]
TOTAL　　　　SCORE

Healing

[　　] + [　　] + [　　] + [　　] + [　　] +
Item 16　　Item 34　　Item 52　　Item 70　　Item 88

[　　] + [　　] + [　　] + [　　] + [　　] =
Item 98　　Item 101　　Item 100　　Item 102　　Item 103

[　　] ÷ 10 = [　　]
TOTAL　　　　SCORE

Tongues

[　　] + [　　] + [　　] + [　　] + [　　] +
Item 17　　Item 35　　Item 53　　Item 71　　Item 89

[　　] = [　　] ÷ 6 = [　　]
Item 99　　TOTAL　　　　SCORE

Interpretation [　　] + [　　] + [　　] + [　　] =
Item 18　　Item 36　　Item 54　　Item 72

[　　] ÷ 4 = [　　]
TOTAL　　　　SCORE

68

Graphing Your Profile

1. For each gift, draw a line across the bar for that gift at the point which corresponds to your SCORE for that gift.

2. For each gift, shade the bar below the line which you have drawn.

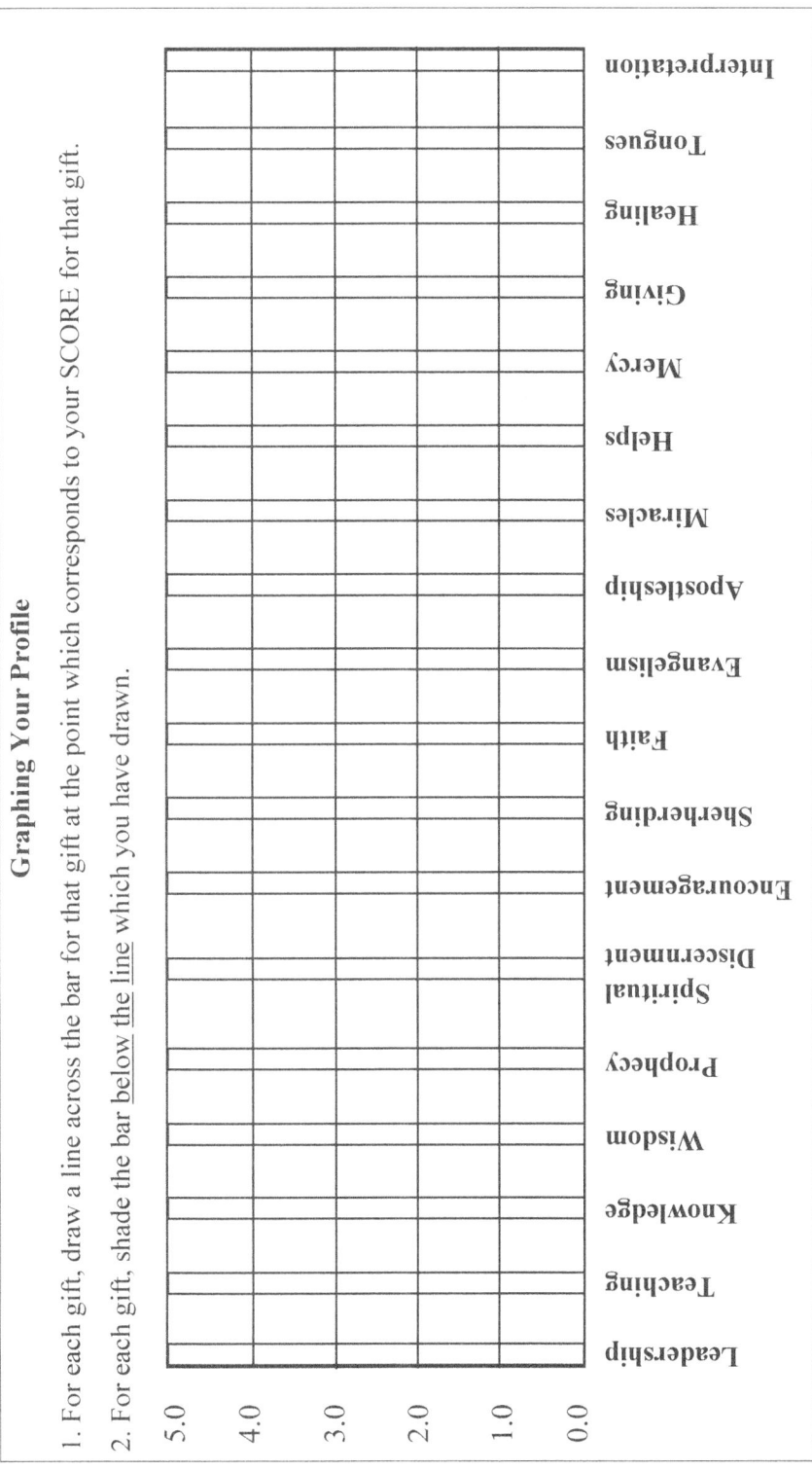

	Leadership	Teaching	Knowledge	Wisdom	Prophecy	Spiritual Discernment	Encouragement	Sherherding	Faith	Evangelism	Apostleship	Miracles	Helps	Mercy	Giving	Healing	Tongues	Interpretation
5.0																		
4.0																		
3.0																		
2.0																		
1.0																		
0.0																		

Definitions/Explanations
of Spiritual Gifts

Leadership/Administration/Government

To set or place over. To be over, to superintend, preside over. To be a protector or guardian, to give aid.
Thayer's Greek-English Lexicon of the New Testament (p. 539)

To guide, as in piloting a ship.
Vines Expository Dictionary of New Testament Words (p. 508)

The ability to direct and guide a church with wise counsel in conducting the ministry God has given. *Spiritual Gifts Inventory* (BSSB, unpublished)

See Acts 6:1-8; Titus 1:5; Acts 15:1-31.

Teaching

The special ability to study God's word and to communicate spiritual truths in such a way that they are relevant to the health and ministry of the church and in a way that others will learn.
Spiritual Gifts Inventory

See Acts 11:22-26.

Knowledge

The ability to discover, understand, clarify, and communicate information that relates to the life, growth, and well-being of the church. *Spiritual Gifts Inventory*

The deeper, more perfect and enlarged knowledge of this religion, such as belongs to the more advanced. *Thayer* (p.119)

70

To come to know, recognize, understand, or to understand completely. *Vines* (p. 637)

See Acts 18:24-28.

Wisdom

Broad and full intelligence, used of the knowledge of very diverse matters. The ability to discourse eloquently of this wisdom. *Thayer* (p. 582)

The ability to gain insight into the practical application of God's truth to specific situations. *Spiritual Gifts Inventory*

The practical application of insight into divine wisdom to our own and to others' lives.
The Interpretation of 1 and 2 Corinthians, Lenski (p. 500)

See Acts 15:1-31.

Prophecy/Prophet

One who speaks forth the word of God. The proclaimer of a divine message. The purpose of this ministry is to edify, to comfort, to encourage the believers (1 Cor. 14:3). Prophecy's effect upon unbelievers was to show that the secrets of a person's heart are known to God, to convict of sin, and to constrain to worship (1 Cor. 14:24-25). *Vine's* (p. 903)

The special ability to receive from God a message and then to communicate that message to others through a divinely anointed utterance. *Spiritual Gifts Inventory*

See Acts 11:27-30.

Spiritual Discernment

The ability to discriminate between that which is of the Holy Spirit and that which is not, especially as it pertains to oral testimony. *Vines* (p. 317)

The ability to know which actions and teachings that are claimed to be of God are actually of God (and not human or satanic). *Spiritual Gifts Inventory*

See 1 John 5:1.

Encouragement

The special ability to comfort and encourage others as well as to motivate others to right actions. *Spiritual Gifts Inventory*

To stand alongside another giving support and comfort—to console, to give aid to another. *Vines*

To address, speak to, which may be done in the way of exhortation, entreaty, comfort, instruction—hence encouragement embraces a variety of senses.

See Acts 4:31-37; 9:26-27.

Shepherding/Pastor

Tending herds or flocks—giving tender care and vigilant supervision. *Vines* (p. 849)

The overseers of Christian assemblies. *Thayer* (p. 527)

Exercising care and control over others. The ability to build up,

equip, and guide Christians toward spiritual maturity.
Spiritual Gifts Inventory

See 1 Peter 5:1-4; Ephesians 4:11-16.

Faith

The special ability to discern and affirm God's will and purposes in the world and to be a part of His intervention through prayer and the Spirit's power. *Spiritual Gifts Inventory*

The supernatural ability to perceive the will of God and to commit one's self to doing it.

See Acts 8:26-40.

Evangelism/Evangelist

A messenger of good. A preacher of the gospel. *Vines* (p. 384)

The ability to comprehend the lost condition of people in the world and to present Christ effectively so that persons will accept salvation in Jesus. *Spiritual Gifts Inventory*

See Acts 8:4ff.

Apostleship/Apostle

A sending, a mission. One sent on a mission. *Thayer* (p. 65)

The ability to share the gospel in special ways. These are persons who are sent by God with His message of reconciliation.
Spiritual Gifts Inventory

See Acts 9:1-22.

Miracles

Power, inherent ability, used of works of a supernatural origin and character, such as could not be produced by natural agents and means. *Vines* (p.757)

The special ability to serve as human intermediaries through which God works to bring about events that cannot be explained by natural law. *Spiritual Gifts Inventory*

See Acts 19:11-12.

Helps/Service

Abilities for rendering helpful services to the destitute, the sick, the persecuted, the troubled. Services for the sake of services. *The Interpretation of 1 and 2 Corinthians,* Lenski (p. 540)

The ability to render service to benefit and help others, this being the only motive—all compulsion being absent. Helpful, voluntary service motivated by obedience to God as a servant.

The ability and desire to recognize day-to-day needs of others and to meet those needs personally. Spiritual Gifts Inventory Assistance rendered, especially to the weak and needy. *Vines* (p. 317)

The ministrations of the deacons who have care of the poor and the sick. *Thayer* (p. 50)

See Acts 6:1-8; Philippians 2:25-30.

Mercy

The outward manifestation of pity. Mercy is the act of God on behalf of needy persons. *Vines* (p. 742)

The merciful person is to greet every opportunity for a merciful deed as a great find that makes him jubilant. Grudging mercy is not to be his manner of doing. We are to show mercy with great joy (literally, hilarity). *Romans*, Lenski (p. 765)

Kindness or good will toward the miserable and afflicted, joined with a desire to relieve them. *Thayer* (p. 203)

The ability to feel sympathy and compassion for and to meet actively the needs of persons who suffer distress and crises from the physical, mental, or emotional problems.
Spiritual Gifts Inventory

See Acts 9:36.

Giving

To give a share of, to impart (meta, with), as distinct from giving. The sense means to do more than to give one's physical or material goods. It encompasses that, but moves beyond it to indicate a sharing with others so as to spend or pour out one's life for others. Paul used this term in Romans 1:11 when he wrote that he wanted to see the Roman Christians so he could impart (give) some spiritual gift to them. He did not mean that he would give them a gift, but rather, that he would share or impart his gift or gifts for their benefit. *Vines* (p. 489)

To share a thing with anyone. *Thayer* (p. 404)

The ability and desire to contribute material resources to others and the Lord's work with liberality and cheerfulness.
Spiritual Gifts Inventory

See Acts 4:36-37; Romans 1:11.

Healing

Divinely imparted gifts of physical and spiritual healing. Carries with it the concept of wholeness, being made whole.
Vines (p.543-544)

The God-given ability to help others regain physical, mental, or spiritual health through the direct action of God.
Spiritual Gifts Inventory

See Acts 16:16-18.

Tongues

The special ability to speak to God through Spirit-inspired utterances and/or to receive and communicate an immediate message of God to His people through Spirit-inspired utterances.
Spiritual Gifts Inventory

The supernatural gift of speaking in another language without having learned it.   *Vines* (p. 1165)

Language spoken by persons who in rapt ecstasy are no longer quite masters of their own reason and consciousness. They pour forth their glowing spiritual emotions in strange utterances, rugged, dark, disconnected, quite unfitted to instruct or to influence the minds of others.   *Thayer* (p. 188)

See Acts 10:44-48 and Acts 19:1-7.

Interpretation

To unfold the meaning of what is said, explain, expound.
Thayer (p. 147)

The conversion of what is unintelligible into what is intelligible.
Theological Dictionary of the New Testament (p. 665)

The ability to convey a rational account of what was spoken in a tongue. *The Interpreter's Dictionary of the Bible* (p. 672)

[Although the gift of interpretation is mentioned, no specific instance of the gift is given in the text of the New Testament. Some think that the explanation offered by Peter (Acts 2:13ff.) on the Day of Pentecost was interpretation.]

Notes and Observations

Reflect on the gifts God has given for us to use in ministry.

Where Gifts Can Be Used in Deacon Ministry Teams

To offer you some ideas for how various gifts can be used, the following suggestions are offered.

Avenues of Using Gifts

Following is a partial list of avenues that believers can pursue in using their gifts in ministry. A complete list cannot be developed because that list is limited only to the needs that arise and the imagination to meet them. Many of these are avenues of ministry for deacons.

The ministry suggestions are grouped under four major headings that capsule the primary ministry areas of a church's work: *Service, Teaching, Worship, Witness*. The gifts necessary to these ministry areas are listed as well.

It is difficult to be definitive with this grouping because some gifts find expression in more than one ministry area. For instance, encouragement can be used in serving as well as in worship; faith can be used in worship as well as in witness. These suggestions are provided to give some direction in ministry and to stimulate ideas for ministry. Studying these will generate additional ideas for ministry in each of these areas.

1. Service: **helps/service, mercy, giving, healing, leadership/ governments/administration**

Hospital ministry; benevolence committee; counseling; support groups; work with the divorced, widowed, orphaned, or neglected; work with older people; family ministries; disaster relief; ministry to homebound.

2. Teaching: **wisdom, knowledge, teaching**

Bible teaching; leadership training; leading discipleship groups;

new member training; providing Bible lessons and sermons for shut-ins; retreat leadership; guiding mission study groups; leading marriage enrichment groups.

3. *Worship:* prophecy, spiritual discernment, encouragement, shepherding

Giving devotionals; preaching; worship team; usher committee; Lord's Supper committee; Christian growth conferences; baptismal committee; music ministry; giving testimony; prayer group leader; worship leader.

4. *Witness:* faith, evangelism, apostleship, miracles, tongues, interpretation

Outreach; personal witnessing; hospital ministry; jail/prison ministry; guiding mission teams, church planting, preaching evangelistic messages; taking the gospel to language groups; Christian service corps; and other short-term mission projects.

These are only suggestive representations of where some gifts can be used. The place where gifts can be used is limited on by the call of God and our willingness to obey.

Complete the activity on the following page. It will help you process your profile and determine where God is calling you to serve in or through the Body of Christ, the church.

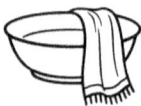 Gordon Cosby has identified three indicators of a call to ministry:

♦ You have a feeling of *Eureka*-I've found it!

♦ You see visions and dream dreams.

♦ You can't stop talking about it.

What are your primary gifts? (Refer to page 69.) List the top five gifts here:

Do these best equip you for ministry in the church to the Body or through the Body to the world?

What are some of your natural talents?

What are some of the skills you have developed?

Do you have a particular passion for some avenue of ministry? What ministry creates excitement in you?

Your ministry will probably be found in the arena where all of these elements in your life converge. Look at your spiritual gifts, your talents, your skills, and your passion. Where are you equipped to serve in the Body? To what ministry do you feel God leading you?

Session 5

Organizing Deacons for Ministry

Deacon ministry is one of the more complex areas of ministry in the church. **Deacons address every area of pastoral ministry— bereavement, administration, hospital ministry, family ministry, spiritual development, evangelism, new member orientation—you name it, they do it.** Because of the complexity of deacon ministry, organizing deacon ministry is also a complex process. The chart on the following page details some of the components that must be addressed when organizing for deacon ministry.

This chapter and the following three explore all these components of organizing deacons for ministry.

Statement of Deacon Ministry Purpose

A statement of purpose is the first requirement for any effective deacon ministry. A clear understanding of purpose provides direction. Notice from the New Testament how a clear understanding of purpose provided dynamic direction in the ministries of Jesus and Paul.

Jesus was the most purposeful person that ever lived. In speaking of necessity of service for greatness in the kingdom of God, Jesus said that He *came not to be served, but to serve and to give His life a ransom for many* (Mk. 10:45). Because He knew who He was and why He was, He was able to live intentionally. This determined His choices and actions.

Components of Deacon Ministry	
Deacon Ministry Purpose Statement	**Why do what we do?**
Needs of Audience	**Who is the target audience for this ministry? What are their needs?**
Leadership	**Who can provide leadership to this ministry? What gifts are needed by this/these person/s to lead this ministry?**
Strategies	**What do we do to fulfill the purpose of our ministry/ calling and to meet the needs of our church and community?**
Organization	**How can we organize to effectively meet the needs? What structure is required?**
Resources	**What resources will help meet the needs we have identified?**

When tempted, He could resist (Mt. 4:1-11). When the crowd tried to make Him an earthly king (Jn. 6:15), He was able to resist because that was not in keeping with His mission. When told by Peter that He could not die (Mt. 16:22), He heard the voice of the tempter, and was able to resist the temptation to go in a different direction.

Luke revealed the intentionality of Jesus when He stated, and it came to pass, when the time was come that He should be received up, He steadfastly set His face to go to Jerusalem (Lk 9:51). He went to Jerusalem to achieve His destiny and the purpose of the Father. Knowing His purpose kept Jesus focused on the priorities of His life? Have the deacons of your church been focused on the priorities of a purposeful ministry?

The apostle Paul gave a very succinct statement of purpose in his letter to the Colossians...

Now I rejoice in what was suffered for you, and I fill up in my flesh what is still lacking in regard to Christ's afflictions, for the sake of His body, which is the church. I have become its servant by the commission God gave me to present to you the word of God in its fullness. The mystery that has been kept hidden for ages and generations, but is now disclosed to the saints. To them God has chosen to make known among the Gentiles the glorious riches of this mystery, which is Christ in you, the hope of glory. ***We proclaim Him, admonishing and teaching everyone with all wisdom, so that we may present everyone perfect in Christ. To this end I labor, struggling with all His energy, which so powerfully works in me*** (Col. 1:24-29).

Paul's statement of purpose was to present everyone perfect in Christ! The decisions he made and the actions he performed took him step by step toward that goal of presenting every person perfect (complete) in Christ.

What if your deacon ministry adopted this as its mission or vision statement? What areas of ministry should be or would be developed to present every person complete in Christ?

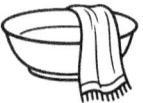 **Someone stated, "Show me your calendar and your check book and I will tell you what your priorities are."**

1. List the ministries performed by your deacons in the last twelve months.

2. List the topics discussed by your deacons in the last twelve months.

3. As you evaluate these listings, can you say your deacons are aimed toward a single purpose? If so, what is that single purpose? Write a statement of purpose for your deacon ministry.

Needs of the Audience

To be complete in Christ is to be like Christ. In Luke 2:52, we read of Jesus, He increased in wisdom and stature and in favor with God and man. Jesus developed in four dimensions—intellectual/emotional, physical, spiritual and social. We can use these four areas of ministry suggested in Luke 2:52 to focus our purpose of presenting everyone perfect in Christ—of helping persons mature in Him.

These four areas of personal development could be the four broad areas of your deacon ministry. Deacon ministry should be balanced. A deacon ministry targeted at these areas could look like this diagram.

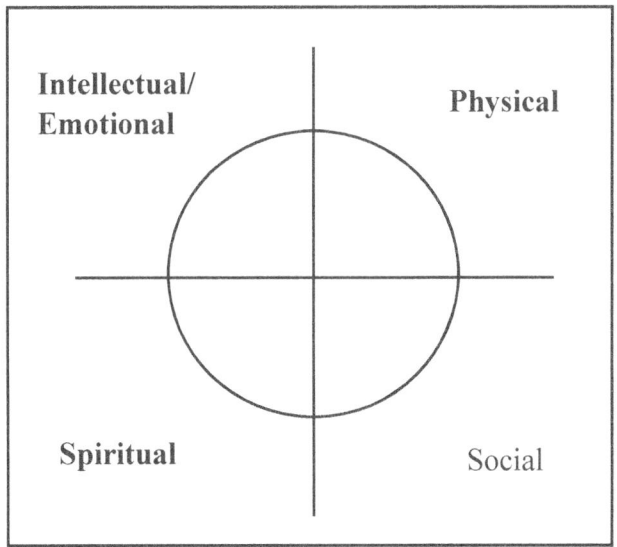

Balance means addressing the needs of persons in all of the areas of development. Yet, a balanced ministry doesn't mean that all needs will receive equal time, weight, or energy. Different needs are greater at different periods of a person's life. For example, if a church member just lost his or her mother in death, a money management seminar is not the pressing need. They need some-one to help them grieve over the loss of their loved one.

Balanced deacon ministry will address all areas, but will do so on a priority basis. The following process can be used to help the deacons identify needs of the church and community from which they will establish their priorities for ministry. (A variety of forms are suggested throughout this process. They can be used or modified in format and delivery vehicle to help you discover priority needs for ministry.)

The *first step* is to identify the present ministries of your church. Develop a list of ministries offered by your church. You might use a simple form like this:

Ministries Our Church Offer

Intellectual/emotional needs :

Physical needs :

Spiritual needs :

Social needs :

The *next step* in identifying priority ministries for your deacons is to survey the entire membership to identify their ministry needs. Consider a survey of the membership with some sample needs such as the following and any others you can identify. The object is to discover the needs that exist and that are not being met.

Needs Survey Sheet

The deacons of our church wish to know if our church is ministering to your needs and the needs within our community. Please complete this survey and return it as soon as possible.

Please check any need you feel our church should meet.

_____Coping with stress

_____Relationships

_____Managing money

_____Prayer needs

_____Bible study skills

_____Childcare

_____Care for aging parents

_____Alcohol and drug abuse

_____Parenting problems

_____New member assimilation

_____Divorce recovery

_____Grief recovery

_____Shut-in ministry

_____Hospital ministry

_____Reclamation of inactive members

_____Disaster relief

After the ministries your church offers have been listed in the four areas (intellectual/emotional, physical, spiritual, and social) and the needs of the congregation surveyed, the next step is to compile the needs listed by the congregation. This list should be categorized according to the four areas you have previously used. The form below will help in this process.

Needs Our Church Identified for Attention

Intellectual/emotional needs :

Physical needs :

Spiritual needs :

Social needs :

Is your church meeting members' needs? If your ministry is balanced, needs are being met. Most churches emphasize what they perceive is needed. The programs of your church have been developed to address perceived needs. Deacons can develop ministries to meet the needs that are not the focus of other program ministries.

The **next step** in identifying the priority ministries for deacons is to compare the list of ministries offered by the church and the summary list of needs identified by the membership for attention. This comparison will reveal needs that are not currently being met. The unmet needs the church identified will be the basis for the priority ministries of the deacons. The following form will help you compile the list of unmet needs.

Unmet Needs Our Church Identified

Intellectual/emotional needs :

Physical needs :

Spiritual needs :

Social needs :

The process of surveys and compilation will result in a fairly accurate list of unmet needs in the church and community. From this list, the future ministries of the deacons may be selected. The list of unmet needs is the basis for the ministry choices to be listed on the Personal Gifts Profile (page 121).

It should be accepted that deacons will not try to do everything. As we proceed, you will see how to select priority ministries for deacons.

Feasibility Factors

Many needs will be discovered in the church or even in the larger community. Not all these needs can or even should be addressed by your deacon ministry. Certain feasibility factors come into play that help you make decisions about the needs that your deacon ministry can address.

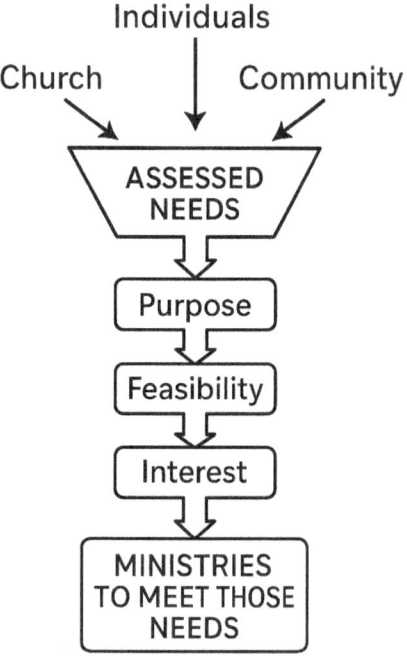

Malcom Knowles created the process that helps institutions see the flow of the program (ministry) development process. This chart is an adaptation of that process.

Imagine the various needs flowing into funnels at the top of the grid. They come from individual lives, from the organizational church, and from the community in which the church is located. These form a collective set of needs for the deacons to consider. As these travel through the assessment process to determine if they are needs that should be addressed, they must pass through a series of grids or filters. Those that pass all the filters become viable needs for consideration in deacon ministry.

The first filter that must be passed is the ***purpose statement***. Consider how those needs relate to the purpose of the church and the deacons. For instance, someone may want to find a spouse and get married. Deacons must decide if the church or the deacons are existing to be a dating service for singles. How that fits your purpose determines if it becomes part of your ministry.

Another filter is the ***existing ministries*** already at work in the church. Many needs reflected in a survey of the church will already be the responsibility of other committees, councils, programs, or groups. It should be noted that deacons are not attempting to absorb other existing ministries under their domain in this approach to deacon ministry. If a need can be met by an existing program or ministry in your church, channel that need to the appropriate group.

Another filter is ***feasibility***. Some needs or ministries are not feasible for the deacons because of limited resources. Resources include space, money, time, church support, staff, and other factors that seem evident when examining a need. The availability of resources can restrict some ministry endeavors.

Leadership can be another limitation. Some needs will involve areas where deacons are not gifted or trained. If ministry demands exceed the capabilities of the deacons, other church members can be enlisted by the deacons as partners in ministry. The concept behind the title of this book is that the deacons lead teams composed from the congregation to meet the needs in the church and beyond. If the membership shows little interest, this will limit the response deacons can make to specific needs.

Selecting Priority Needs

As you study the list of unmet needs of the church and community, needs can be identified that are feasible for deacon ministry. These needs will be the focus of future work for deacons. It is expected that the list might be long. Deacons should not attempt all needs at once. A process of selecting priority needs for ministry must be developed.

The unmet ministry needs that have been identified as feasible are the priority needs for deacon ministry. These should be grouped into four divisions—Service, Teaching, Worship, Witness. Such a division will help in assigning deacons according to their spiritual gifts later. This step translates needs into ministry.

Create a form that lists all the priority needs for deacon ministry. (Note the following example.) When the form you have developed is given to the deacons, instruct them to rank the ministry needs according to their perception of the first, second, and third most pressing ministry needs in the church or community. Compiling these preferences will indicate the priority needs as perceived by the deacons. These priority needs will be the options for deacon ministry selection and the basis for developing deacon ministry teams.

When the deacons have completed their forms, collect them and compile their responses to discover the more pressing needs of the church and community that deacons will address. After this has been done, deacons will be organized to meet those needs.

A word of caution at this point—

All the forms used in this chapter are simply examples of the process of determining priorities for ministry. The forms must be tailored to reflect the needs of your church and community.

Priority Needs for Deacon Ministry

Name: _____

Circle up to three needs you would consider as the most pressing needs in our church or community.

SERVICE

Hospital
Benevolence
Homebound
Caring
Grief
Divorce
Big Bro/Sis
Family Ministry
Security
Disaster Relief

WITNESS

Prospects
Evangelism
Decision Counseling
Member Reclamation

TEACHING

Stewardship
Proclamation
Leadership Development
New Member
        Assimilation

WORSHIP

Lord's Supper
Baptism
Prayer
Worship
Jail Ministry
Greeter
Memorials
Ushers

Notes and Observations

Session 6
Leadership Concepts
for Deacon Ministry

Our concepts of leadership affects our understanding of how deacons meet the needs of a church's membership. Two primary ideas of leadership are generally mentioned in relationship to deacon ministry—positional authority and servant-leader. The leadership style of Jesus offers us a pattern to follow.

The Model Leader

Jesus is our model for leadership. Jesus modeled for us a servant-leader style of leadership. In the upper room at the last supper, Jesus told the disciples that he had given them an example that they were to do as He had done (Jn. 13:15). He had become a servant to them—taking basin and towel washing their feet. They too were to become servants.

Far too few are looking for the basin and towel and far too many are looking for the office marked CEO. Earlier in the ministry of Jesus, a conflict had broken out in the body of the disciples over the request of John and James to sit one on the right and one on the left of Jesus in the Kingdom. Jesus said that greatness in the kingdom was dependent upon the willingness to become a servant (Mark 10:35-45). The path to greatness is the path of servanthood. The ideas of leadership and greatness that Jesus espoused run contrary to the ideas held by the world.

The world's view of greatness is to rise to the pinnacle of the pyramid. Get to the top—become president, CEO, top dog, *numero uno*—any way you can.

The objective is to have as many as possible under you who are servant to you. Jesus' view of greatness is to get to the bottom of an inverted pyramid. The objective is to have as many people above you to whom you are servant. Become a servant— become the servant of all—if you want to become great in the kingdom. Isaiah was clear in contrasting God's ways with ours— As *the heavens are higher than the earth, so are my ways higher than your ways and my thoughts than your thoughts* (Is. 55:9). God turns all our standards of greatness, importance, and ministry up-side-down.

Servant Leadership

Jesus embodied servant-leadership for us. Leaders should support those who are doing ministry—running interference, protecting the schedule from conflicts, finding resources—whatever it takes to assist deacons in performing the ministry God has called them to do.

Leaders in any Christian organization should seek ways to become servants to those with whom they work. Most leadership structures are diagrammed from the top to the bottom.

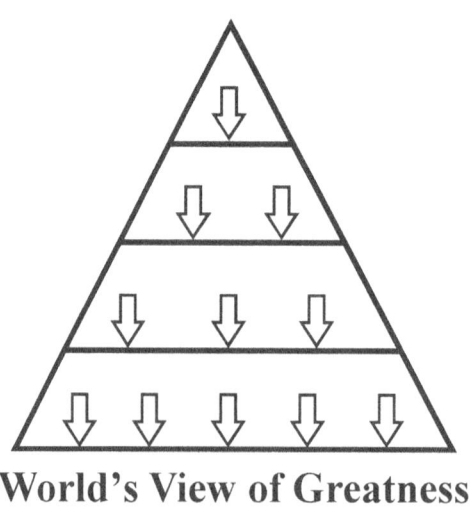

World's View of Greatness

The higher the level of leadership on the chart, the higher the level of authority and power. This model is a line management structure often found in the business world. Directives come down to lower levels who are to act upon those directives.

Christian leadership turns the charts up-side-down. The higher the level of leadership on the chart, the higher the level of authority and power. This model is a line management structure often found in the business world. Directives come down to lower levels who are to act upon those directives. Christian leadership turns the charts up-side-down.

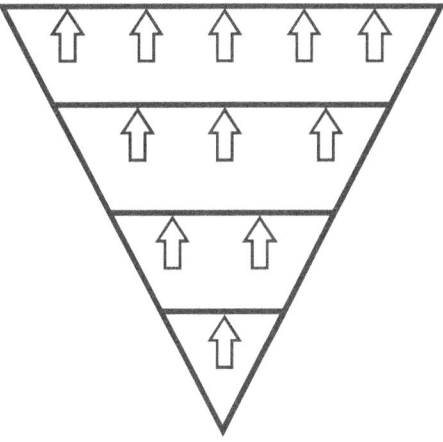

God's View of Greatness

Every level of leadership supports the level above it with authority, teaching, training, modeling, protection, support, and cheerleading. This is exactly what Jesus did with the Twelve. After a year of public ministry, Jesus selected from those who were following Him as Messiah a group of leaders. After praying all night, He selected the Twelve (Lk. 6:12-13). Into these Twelve, Jesus invested His time and attention—equipping them for the leadership roles they were to fulfill in the church. Jesus was an equipper.

Shared Leadership

Leaders in the Christian community must have as their basic leadership model the equipping model of Ephesians 4:11-12—*It was he who gave some to be apostles, some to be prophets, some to be evangelists, and some to be pastors and teachers, to prepare God's people for works of service, so that the body of Christ may be built up.*

Jack Cunningham has made an interesting observation about any leadership model that is devised along a vertical concept—up or down. *Up* suggests that power or authority resides at the top and that dictates come down to others who will carry out those dictates. *Down* might suggest that those below in the servant role have no authority and deserve no accountability.

Another problem with the diagram of deacon ministry that is just up or down is the emphasis upon the individual deacon. Sometimes the weight is too great upon the individual. The expectations can be overpowering and crushing.

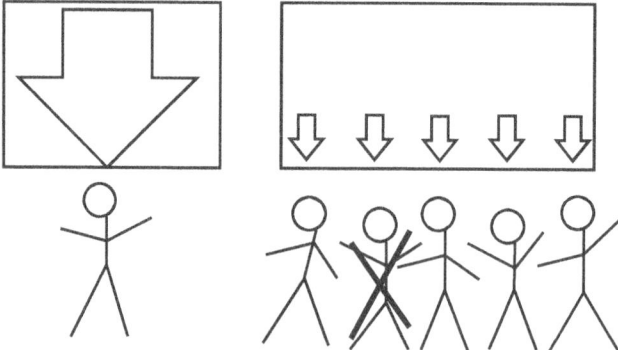

If the weight of leadership rests upon one person only, that person has the great potential of burnout. Should that person move or dropout, the ministry has the possibility of collapsing. If the weight of leading the ministry is shared by many, each individual carries only part of the load of leadership. The burden, then, is lighter on any individual at any one time. If an individual moves or drops out, others can continue the ministry.

Diagrams that portray organization in ways other than top-down structures may better reflect Christian concepts of leadership. In the church, leadership is not simply a matter of ministry flowing from one individual to another—it often flows both ways, in a reciprocal exchange (1 Peter 4:10). Leadership is not confined to a single person. In a Body where every believer is gifted and called to minister, leadership is less about position or authority and more about stepping into a role as the ministry requires at any given moment or situation.

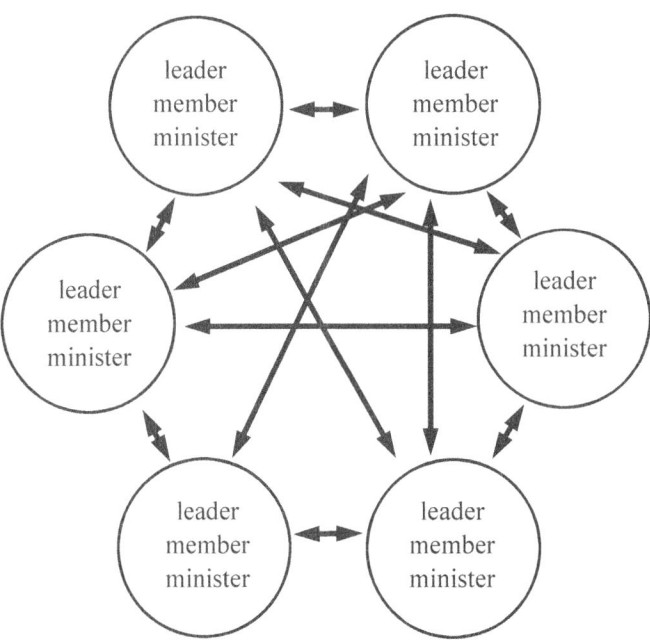

The ministry might best be described as ministry *with* deacons in this model of ministry. The leadership role changes from instance to instance or situation to situation. Depending upon the ministry and the gifts needed, one person might lead one segment and someone else lead another. We do not just have *the* leader—we actually have *many* leaders. Peter expressed this idea in his first letter—*As every man hath received the gift, even so minister the same one to another as good stewards of the manifold grace of God* (1 Pt. 4:10).

Relationships within the Body of Christ, the Church, are **interdependent**. None is self-sufficient. We need one another. The Body will not function as it should unless every member is using his or her gifts in ministry. Paul noted this in his letter to the Ephesians—*From him the whole body, joined and held together by every supporting ligament, grows and builds itself up in love, as each part does its work* (4:16). Each person has a contribution to make to the Body.

In an effective deacon ministry, each deacon is important because each is uniquely gifted to make a contribution to the ministry. The ministry might best be described as ministry with deacons in this model of ministry. The leadership role changes from instance to instance or situation to situation. Depending upon the ministry and the gifts needed, one person might lead one segment and someone else lead another. We do not just have the leader—we actually have many leaders. Peter expressed this idea in his first letter—*As every man hath received the gift, even so minister the same one to another as good stewards of the manifold grace of God* (1 Pt. 4:10).

Relationships within the Body of Christ, the Church, are interdependent. None is self-sufficient. We need one another. The Body will not function as it should unless every member is using his or her gifts in ministry. Paul noted this in his letter to the Ephesians—*From him the whole body, joined and held together by every supporting ligament, grows and builds itself up in love, as each part does its work* (4:16). Each person has a contribution to make to the Body. In an effective deacon ministry, each deacon is important because each is uniquely gifted to make a contribution to the ministry.

Strategies for Meeting Needs

A strategy is a plan of action designed for achieving an objective or a specific goal. The strategies for specific deacon ministries will arise from three primary sources—your purpose statement, the needs of your audience, and the spiritual gifts of the deacons.

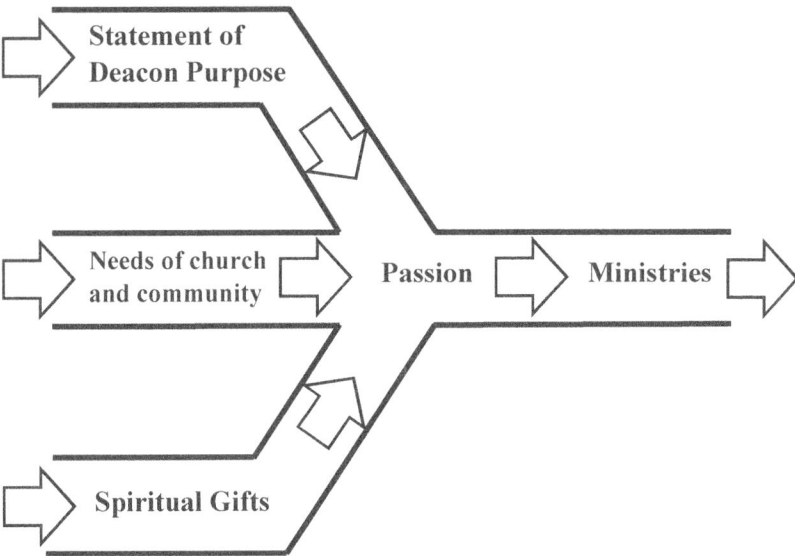

The scope of your ministry will be dictated by the breadth of your purpose statement. Only needs that are consistent with the purpose of deacons should be considered for ministry.

Another necessary element to consider is the needs of the church and community. The purpose of the survey of the membership is to measure their needs and those of the community and expectations of service and help from the church. Some needs may be met by other programs and groups. To know the needs, is to begin to identify areas where deacons might minister.

The final element is the spiritual gifts of the deacons. The gifts are God's method of operation through believers' lives—the indicators of the ministries deacons are to perform and the point of power and joy in service.

Once these elements have been determined, deacons will be organized into ministry teams based on their passion for and calling to a particular ministry. These teams will be responsible for developing ministry strategies to meet the priority needs they have identified. The next two sections guide you through the process of organizing deacons into teams.

Notes and Observations

Session 7

Custom Fit Your Deacon Ministry

Think of organization as a suit of clothes. *One-size-fits-all* is definitely not true for deacon ministry. No one organizational structure is *suit*able for every deacon ministry. But this is also true for *ready-to-wear* or *off-the-rack*.

It might be nice simply to go to the rack and select the proper size and style to fit. Just select the options from an A, B, or C plan for organization—*give us your size, we'll give you a structure to fit*. That just is not going to happen in most places.

This has been somewhat the style in the past. Organization was often simply selected *off-the-rack*—you were given several organizational structures and you were told to chose the one that fit your size. If you had 1-12 deacons, you chose model "A", if you had 13-25, you chose model "B" and so forth. It would be nice if it were that simple. Truth is—deacon ministry is not simple—it is complex.

The Deacon Family Ministry Plan has been a good attempt at moving deacons from a purely administrative/business orientation to a ministry orientation, but it is still a *one-size-fits-all* model for ministry. This approach to deacon ministry neglects the unique giftedness of each deacon, each deacon body, and even each church. Regardless of gifts, deacons are expected to perform the same ministry.

Attempts are sometimes made to duplicate the shapes and styles of deacon ministry from one church to another. A leader or leaders in one church see what another church is doing and tries to follow the same patterns of organization and ministry. This *same-as-another* approach is one of the surest and quickest ways to stifle creativity and effectiveness in deacon ministry.

Every church's deacon ministry has to be *tailor-made*. Deacon ministry will vary from church to church and even from community to community because of the variations of the deacons' spiritual gifts and the needs of the church and community. While certain general characteristics will always exist in deacon ministry (as with human beings—a certain physical conformation will exist), each will have unique characteristics. For a suit to fit well, it must be made to conform not just to the general form of a person but to the specific variations and dimensions of an individual. For deacon ministry to be most effective, it must be tailored to each specific situation.

Thinking in Different Directions

Organization is not merely a superimposed structure. It is tailored according to the preceding factors of purpose, needs of audience, leadership available/required, and strategies.

Besides these factors, others figure into any organizational structure you might design. For instance, the key roles of leaders in a team approach to deacon ministry are coordinating, training, equipping, supporting. Another way of looking at organizational structures might be helpful. Instead of thinking in terms of line (up/down) management models of organizational leadership, diagram structures in another way to communicate a different orientation to leadership and ministry roles.

Because organizational structures will be developed to reflect your specific situations, we cannot present models A, B, and C.

But...

what we can do is to show some patterns that might be helpful in developing your own deacon ministry's organizational structures.

The following diagram provides an overview of a multiple-team ministry. Your deacon body might be small or large, but the elements involved in this structure will be involved in your deacon ministry.

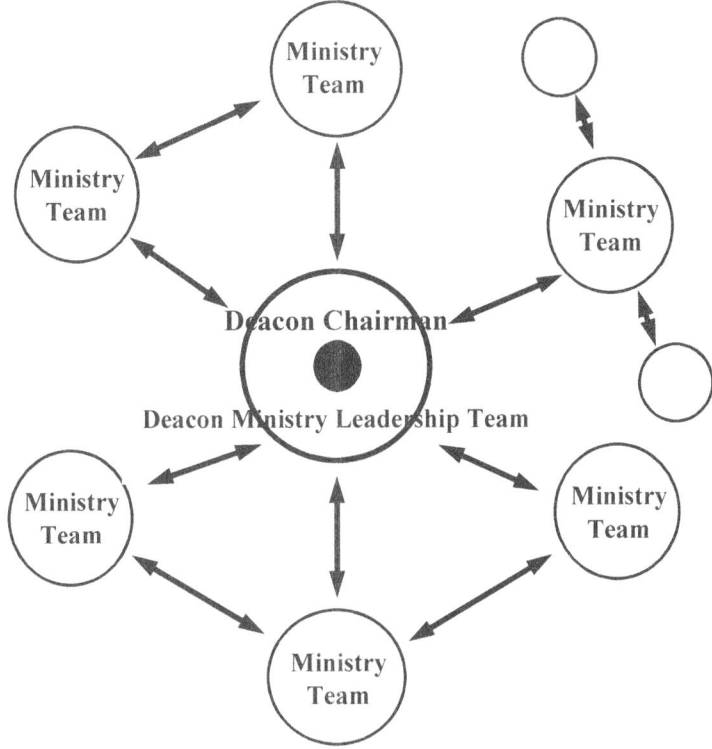

A multiple team structure calls for a different approach to organization. For instance, any situation that has multiple ministries requires greater attention to coordination and planning than a smaller organization. Coordination can be accomplished in a couple of ways. The chairman of deacons can perform the task or a representative leadership team can be formed. As long as a deacon ministry has only a few ministry teams, the deacon chairman can probably coordinate the ministries. As ministry teams proliferate, a leadership team is almost a necessity.

An organizational configuration like the one above might depict more accurately a multiple team model. This configuration brings new ways of looking at the roles of leadership.

♦ The leader of the deacon ministry becomes a coordinator, a player/coach, an equipper.

♦ As the deacon ministry grows, a leadership team will probably be formed to perform functions of planning and coordination.

♦ The model suggests a degree of equality and authority among the teams.

♦ Teams are highly autonomous, yet accountable.

♦ Teams are formed around calling, ministry, and gifts of its members—deacons and other church members as needed.

♦ Some of the teams are connected with information and tasks, maybe even with common members.

♦ Some teams function apart from or with little relations with other teams.

♦ Some teams are large—some are small.

The deacon ministry leader is at the center of the diagram. The circle around the leader is the **D**eacon **L**eadership **T**eam. This leadership team coordinates the overall ministry efforts of the deacon ministry of the church.

The Deacon Leadership Team

The following positions comprise the leadership team to coordi-nate the various ministries to be offered by the deacons—chairman, vice-chairman, secretary/treasurer, service coordinator, teaching coordinator, worship coordinator, witness coordinator. The purpose of this leadership team is to ***coordinate*** the minis-tries performed. Ministry coordinators (service, teaching, wor-ship, witness) will be needed only if more than one or two ministries in a particular area are to be attempted. If only one or two ministries are performed, the team leaders for those ministries can serve as representatives on the leadership team.

The deacon leadership is selected by election from the general body of deacons. It is recommended that the ministry coordinators have spiritual gifts and interests in the ministry area they coordinate. It should also be noted that the vice-chairman usually becomes the chairman in the following year. This selection without election ensures carryover from one year to the next. Since some teams are on-going, continuity in team leadership is helpful to the effectiveness of the ministry.

Responsibilities of Deacon Leadership Team Members

The following leadership positions define needed functions in deacon team ministry. Whether each position is needed or can be combined, is to be determined by the size of the deacon body and the needs of the church fellowship.

The following list of responsibilities of deacon leadership positions are meant to be a beginning point for developing a team ministry with the deacons. You might wish to change these to reflect more accurately your specific situation. However you define your deacon leadership positions, the concept of guiding ministry teams with diverse responsibilities is the focus.

Chairman

The chairman is the presiding officer of the deacons. This person coordinates all deacon ministry in conjunction with the pastor. Responsibilities include:

1. Presiding over all general deacon meetings (usually held monthly).

2. Planning and leading deacons' meetings when held.

3. Guiding the deacons in developing or reviewing the deacon ministry purpose statement.

4. Guiding the process of need identification (as outlined in previous session).

5. Guiding deacon ministry teams to provide the ministries desired.

6. Serving as a representative of deacons to other ministries within the church.

Vice-chairman

The vice-chairman is the chairman-elect of the deacons. This person assists the chairman in the coordination of the deacon work. Responsibilities include:

1. Presiding over all general deacons' meetings when the chairman is absent or delegates the responsibility.

2. Assisting in the planning of deacons' meetings.

3. Maintaining a deacon handbook containing job descriptions of all ministries performed and procedures to perform those ministries that have been approved by the general deacon body.

Secretary-treasurer

The secretary-treasurer records permanent records of all deacons' meetings and procedures for future reference. Responsibilities include:

1. Recording proceedings of all general deacons' meetings

2. Recording proceedings of all deacon leadership meetings.

3. Providing duplication needs and supplies as needed by deacons.

4. Providing any mailing needs as identified by deacons.

5. Providing custodial services for any funds retained by deacons.

Ministry Coordinators (Service, Teaching, Worship, Witness)

The ministry coordinators are responsible for giving leadership to the ministries that deacons wish to perform. Responsibilities include:

1. Convene deacons as a team after the priority area is identified. In this meeting, ministry opportunities are discussed and deacons are encouraged to volunteer for the ministry they wish to perform.

2. Communicate any previously approved job descriptions or procedures that are relevant to ministries chosen.

3. Encourage each ministry team to select a team leader that may be accountable to the ministry coordinator for the work assigned.

4. Conduct periodic meetings with all team leaders to encourage development of job descriptions and procedures that assure quality work.

5.Communicate to the leadership team the need of new job descriptions and procedures that should be approved in the next deacons' meeting.

Deacon Ministry Teams

Ministry teams will be formed by the necessary members to conduct a specific ministry. Depending upon the type and size of the ministry, teams will vary in their composition. For instance, Tom and Marty, along with their wives, have conducted a support ministry for single mothers for a number of years. Tom and Marty are the only deacons required to conduct this particular ministry. Andy, however, heads a ministry team that conducts disaster relief. Andy has seven members on his team. That team coordinates the many aspects of a disaster relief ministry. Other members are recruited to be part of the ministry effort, but only the seven are necessary to plan and coordinate the various events.

A team structure might look like the following diagram...

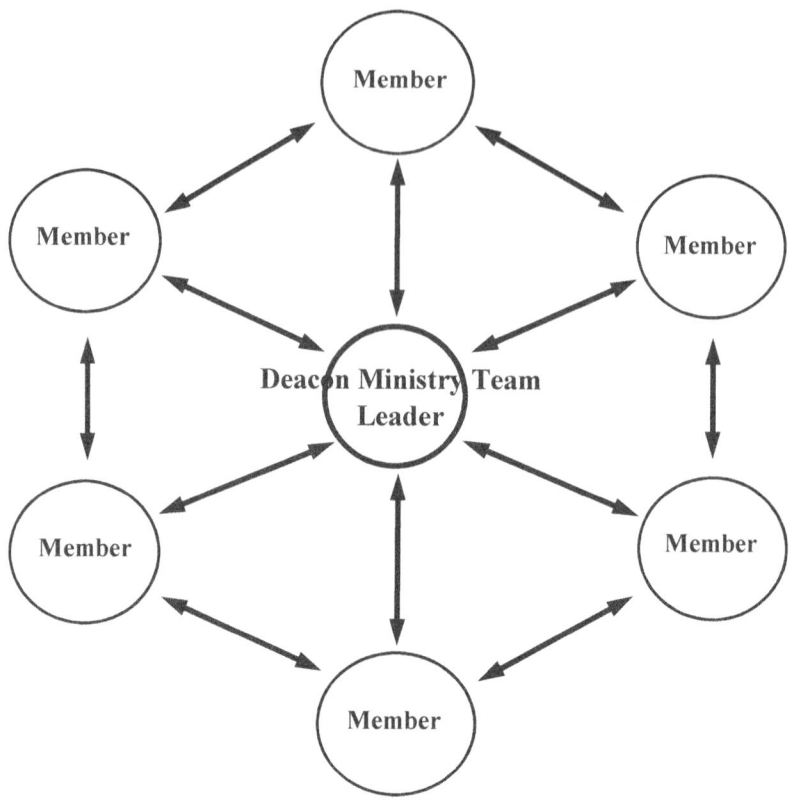

A ministry team will be comprised of as many members as necessary to perform the ministry assignments. Allow us to stress that these teams are *deacon-led* teams. The composition of any team will determined by how many people of the congregation feel called to participate. The various teams will comprise your church's deacon ministry.

Functions of a Deacon Ministry Team

Every deacon ministry team has certain functions that must be conducted if the team is to be successful. The following are the essential functions of a deacon ministry team.

- Coordination
- Record Keeping
- Fellowship
- Ministry

Here's an overview of these primary functions of a deacon ministry team:

Coordination

Coordination is bringing together various parts and factors of a team into a harmonious relationship. Some things involved in a ministry team are members, resources, equipment, schedules, events, relationships, planning, and leadership. Coordination helps the team train, fellowship and minister effectively.

Record Keeping

Accurate records can be an important tool for evaluating and planning the team's work. They also can be a primary source of key information about team members and the ministry performed.

Fellowship

Fellowship is the dynamic that we refer to as *koinonia—that which is held in common.* Fellowship results from the common experiences that bond a group together. Through fellowship, openness, trust, mutual caring and support are experienced. Fellowship is generally thought of as the social events the group does together, but these events are simply occasions that build genuine Christian fellowship. The basis for our fellowship is faith in Christ. We also share other things in common—our gifts, love for one another, and ministry. Some of the greatest fellowship is the fellowship of labor. Mission teams might last only for a short term, for instance. But bonds are formed that are lifelong.

Ministry

A deacon team is organized for ministry. Practical solutions to needs should be the purpose of the ministry team. Accountability to the deacons on a monthly basis reminds teams of their responsibility for action.

Consider forming some of the following teams to conduct the necessary ministries of your church to its members and to the community. And this list is merely suggestive. The teams that will be formed by your church will be as varied as the gifts and calling of your deacons and members

- Proclamation Team
- New Member Assimilation Team
- Leadership Development Team
- Hospital Visitation Team
- Grief Recovery Team
- Member Reclamation Team
- Evangelism Team
- Disaster Relief Team
- Family Ministry Team
- Ministry of Caring Team
- Prospect Visitation Team
- Decision Counseling Team
- Benevolence Team
- Homebound Team
- Divorce Recovery Team
- Security Team
- Stewardship Team
- Baptism Team
- Lord's Supper Team

- Prayer Team
- Worship Team
- Usher Team
- Greeters Team
- Memorial Team
- Missions Team
- Jail Ministry Team

Teams will form as necessary according to need and calling.

Control/Freedom Issues in Organization

In organizing deacon ministry around teams, one of the key issues becomes one of control. If we try to exert control over all the events, actions, and persons in a deacon ministry, we might very well stifle what God is trying to do. When God has freedom to work, our structures and charts might very well go out the window. The disciples tried to exercise a degree of control when they came to Jesus telling of some person who was doing ministry, but who was not connected to their group. Jesus said to leave the person alone—*For he that is not against us is for us* (Mark 9:40).

In the book of Acts, the church at Jerusalem kept trying to control what was happening as the early church was dispersed by persecution. Every time they heard that a new or different group had received the gospel, they sent envoys to investigate the situation. The gospel kept breaking out all over the Roman Empire. It went to the Samaritans (Acts 8). It went to a Roman centurion (Acts 10). It went to Gentiles to the north (Acts 11). In each situation, investigation and an accounting were required by the Jerusalem church. If it were up to the apostles, the gospel would never have gone beyond Jerusalem. But God had other plans. Whatever we do, our structures must align with His will,

The Jerusalem conference (Acts 15) must have been a riot. Can't you just imagine the control freaks of the Jerusalem church running around with their organizational charts showing lines of authority trying to straighten out the conferees. They must have gone ballistic when Paul and Barnabbas stood up and told about the churches they established in Asia Minor. You can almost hear the chartmasters saying, "You can't do that. Who authorized that? That's not on our charts! *You're* not even on our charts! Did any of you here give them permission to preach the word in Asia?"

Two concerns are at work in organizing for a deacon ministry using teams—

1. Freedom to respond to God's call to ministry.

Deacons will exercise their spiritual gifts in many different ministries as needs arise in the membership. As deacons use their gifts, many avenues of ministry will open to them and most of those ministries are not on anyone's charts. Deacons must have the freedom to exercise their gifts as God gives opportunity.

2. Order to contain the chaos that could result from lack of coordination and communication.

Paul's admonition at the conclusion of his passage on public worship might serve us well—*let all things be done decently and in order* (1 Cor. 14:40). While freedom must be provided to keep from inhibiting the spontaneity and dynamic of ministry, some elements of coordination and accountability must be allowed. It is interesting that Paul always came back after his missionary journeys and gave an accounting of his ministry to the Jerusalem and Antioch churches.

Accountability is a necessary part of our stewardship. Deacon ministry teams have an accountability to the larger deacon body. Deacons' meetings can become opportunities to

114

share victories, pray for concerns, coordinate the deacon ministry, and encourage one another.

A tension will always exist between these two concerns. The tension is a healthy tension and should be celebrated—not merely tolerated.

Organization should be flexible or fluid—it will change as needed at any given time. Organization will be a mixture of long-term, static structures and short-term structures. At any one point, a deacon ministry will have some on-going structures and some short-term structures. Avoiding the *organization-as-constant-structures* thinking will help us remain on the cutting edge of organizing to meet needs. Ruts will be avoided. Our ministry structures can stay focused on achieving their purposes.

Notes and Observations

Notes and Observations

Session 8

Assigning Deacons to Ministry Teams

How deacons are assigned to ministry teams will determine each deacon's ownership of the ministry responsibility. In some churches, the deacon leadership will appoint the deacons to assignments. Consideration is given for gifts, interests, talents, and skills. While leaders may have this authority, deacons work better when they own the choices of the ministries they perform.

In the next few pages, a process of guiding all deacons into a choice of work is developed.

Beginning the Ministry Selection Process

The following chart might communicate how we will determine the ministries that deacons will perform during the coming year. Each of the three elements—1) deacon purpose statement, 2) needs of the church and community, and 3) personal spiritual gifts—are crucial to selecting ministries. You might wish to review the text in the section, "Strategies for Meeting Need," on page 101. No ministry should be selected contrary to the reason deacons serve. No ministry should be considered that does not address a specific need. No ministry should be considered that does not have spiritually gifted leadership. Consider this flow of components whenever ministries are being developed and chosen.

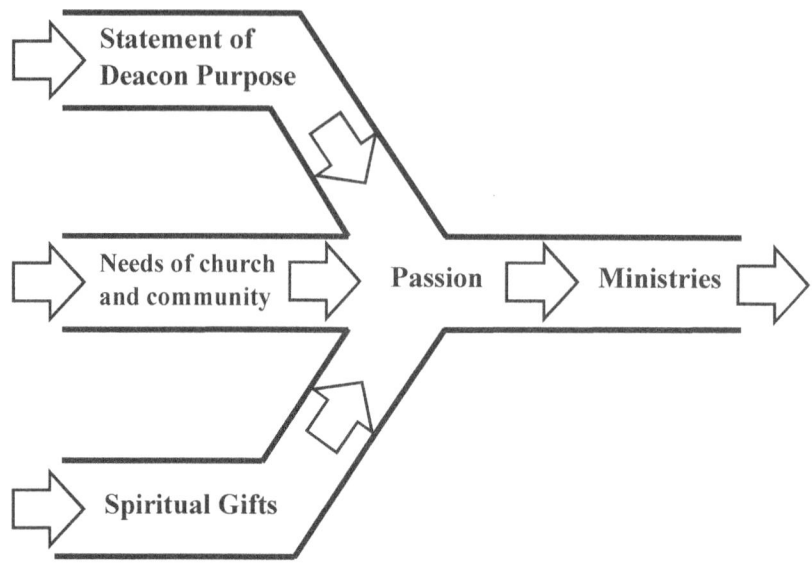

Identifying the Purpose of Deacon Ministry

The initial need of deacons as they organize for a new year is to agree upon their purpose for ministry during the coming year. If you have previously approved a purpose or ministry statement for deacons, share this statement with the entire group. Reminding everyone that deacons serve as overseers of ministry is most important. If no previous purpose statement has been approved, take time to discuss what deacons believe their purpose to be. Continue this discussion until consensus is achieved.

Identifying Personal Interests in Ministry Needs

Ministry needs should have been identified under the leadership of the deacon chairman using the process outlined on pages 101-102. Ministries identified for consideration as deacon ministry need to be listed on the Personal Gifts Profile (p. 121). These ministry needs are to be separated into four areas: Service, Teach-

118

ing, Worship, and Witness. Each individual should be given a copy of the Personal Gifts Profile on which to indicate his preferences. At this point, each deacon should circle any ministry that might interest him.

Knowing the ministries of interest to a deacon is important. Some crisis experienced in the past might sharpen a deacon's desire to serve in a particular area of work. Past experience in certain ministries will also increase a desire to serve. Allowing personal choice under God's leadership will enhance the sense of joy and commitment in ministry.

Administering the Spiritual Gifts Inventory

The Spiritual Gifts Inventory is a good basis for determining a general type of ministry a deacon might enjoy. (The Spiritual Gifts Inventory is found on page 59.) A preferred time to administer the Spiritual Gifts Inventory is sometime during the interview process for selection of deacons. The inventory will take about an hour to administer to the typical group.

Deacons who have taken the inventory previously should consider taking it again. While our gifts might not change, our understanding, perception, and knowledge of our spiritual gifts or our understanding of God's work in our lives might change. Taking the inventory each year will not be too often. Consider an orientation meeting to be held one month prior to deacons beginning a new year of service as a time to administer this inventory to the deacons. At the very least each time a deacon rotates into active status with the deacon body, the inventory should be taken again.

The spiritual gifts that "spike" above all the others should be considered in ministry selection. The combination of these gifts will provide indicators of ministries that should be explored by a particular deacon. While a rating of all gifts could be considered, generally the top five gifts will indicate a tendency toward one of the four areas of ministry: Service, Teaching, Witness, Worship. This indication of a ministry area is all we are concerned with at this point.

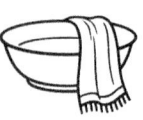 **What are your primary spiritual gifts? Refer to your previous response on page 80. List the top five gifts here for your convenience:**

1.

2.

3.

4.

5.

The Personal Gifts Profile received from each deacon at this orientation meeting might look something like the form on the next page. The ministries listed on this form are simply representative ministries. Your specific list will vary according to the needs that your deacon body identifies from your church and community.

Personal Gifts Profile

Name:_____ Date:_____

Recall that Gordon Cosby identified three indicators of a call to ministry: 1) You have a feeling of *Eureka*-I've found it!

2) You see visions and dream dreams.

3) You can't stop talking about it.

Do you have a particular passion for some avenue of ministry? What is it?

Circle the ministries below that interest you.

SERVICE

Hospital
Benevolence
Homebound
Caring
Grief
Divorce
Big Bro/Sis
Family Ministry
Security
Disaster Relief

WITNESS

Prospects
Evangelism
Decision Counseling
Member Reclamation

TEACHING

Stewardship
Proclamation
Leadership Development
New Member
    Assimilation

WORSHIP

Lord's Supper
Baptism
Prayer
Worship
Jail Ministry
Greeter
Memorials
Ushers

Scoring Deacons Into Ministry Areas

The purpose of this scoring is to place each deacon in a specific ministry area. A Personal Gifts Profile Score Sheet (see example on the next page) should be used to score each deacon. A deacon's score is determined by scoring one (1) point for each gift in a particular area of ministry (Service, Teaching, Worship, Witness—see pages 78-79 for review) and one (1) point for each preferred ministry to which the deacon feels an interest or calling (see next page). All these points will be added together to get a total number of points for each deacon in the four areas of ministry. All four ministry areas are scored for each deacon. Note the following sample on the next page:

Personal Gifts Profile
Score Sheet

Name:_____ **Date:**_____

Directions:

1. Count the number of ministries you have circled in each ministry area and record the score.

2. Count the number of spiritual gifts you have listed according to ministry areas.

3. Add the scores together and see which ministry area has the highest score. You should look for your ministry in that area.

	Worship	**Witness**
Number of ministries preferred	_____	_____
Number of gifts listed	_____	_____
Total score	_____	_____

	Service	**Teaching**
Number of ministries preferred	_____	_____
Number of gifts listed	_____	_____
Total score	_____	_____

Ministry for which I have volunteered this year:

_____

The area with the highest score is the area to which the deacon is assigned. If two or more areas have the same score, the deacon himself should select the area of preference. If the deacon prefers an area other than the one the process has selected, he should be allowed to serve in his area of preference. The result should be a list of deacons identified for each of the four areas of ministry.

Identifying Specific Ministry Assignments

The results of scoring each deacon will be shared. From this information, deacons are encouraged to group themselves into the four areas (**Service**, **Teaching**, **Worship**, **Witness**) to select the ministry they wish to perform.

The Ministry Coordinator for a particular ministry area will lead the deacons assigned to his area. Each deacon should join one of four ministry areas. If your deacons do not consider the Ministry Coordinator a position needed at this time, allow a deacon officer to coordinate the organizing of the ministry teams. The officer is to convene the meeting and guide in the process of allowing each deacon to volunteer for the desired ministry.

All ministries should be discussed before anyone volunteers for one. After all ministries are discussed, personal assignments are made on a consensus basis. Each deacon is allowed to volunteer for a ministry assignment. Several factors should be considered in this process:

1. At least two deacons should be assigned to any ministry to be performed. This will encourage accountability and encourage a team spirit. The maximum number is unlimited. Church members may be enlisted by the deacon team for performing this ministry if additional persons are needed.

2. If no one volunteers for a ministry, it should be possible for an inactive deacon or another church member to be assigned and be

responsible to the Ministry Coordinator of the deacons for the ministry. In such cases, this auxiliary leader would not be required to attend deacons meetings, but should give monthly written reports to the Ministry Coordinator.

3. Considered that all ministries are not to be attempted this year. If the number of deacons appears too small to adequately staff some ministries, those ministries may simply be postponed to the next year or referred to church programs for adoption and implementation.

4. Deacons may possibly volunteer for more than one area of ministry. An example might be that one deacon might volunteer for usher and Lord's supper ministries at the same time. Because these two ministries do not conflict with schedules, this can be allowed. However, each deacon should know clearly which ministry has priority and which ministry is a secondary responsibility. Try to avoid overload.

The final result should be a staffing of the ministries to be performed in the coming year. These volunteers compose the teams responsible for each ministry the deacons will perform. These teams will now develop their ministry under authority of and accountability to the entire deacon body.

Organizing Ministry Teams

Deacons volunteering for ministry will convene their team sometime in the next month to organize the ministry. Ministry teams may schedule their meetings at any time, just as any committee of the church might meet. During a team's first meetings, several priorities should be considered:

1. A team leader should be elected. Leadership ability and experience should be considered. The team leader will represent the

ministry to the entire deacon body.

2. Job descriptions should be developed. All changes should be presented to the entire deacon body for approval. This step encourages accountability.

3. Any approved procedures should be reviewed and modified. All changes should be presented to the entire deacon body for approval as well.

4. Any needs of the church in this area should be discussed for adjustments or improvement of the ministry.

5. Any budgetary needs should be identified and channeled through appropriate channels of the church for financing.

6. Any training sessions for deacons should be noted and scheduled.

[It should be noted that the Pastor and other staff are resources for each team that can enhance a proper implementation of ministry. These ministers should be considered part of the teams and included in all phases of their work.]

Monthly Deacons' Meetings

Monthly deacons' meetings are held as usual. Team leaders will bring any job descriptions, policies, procedures, budget needs, calendar dates, or any other team needs to the entire deacon body. Frequent reports of ministry done should also be encouraged to inspire others with the work being conducted. The agenda will include any of the usual items of discussion. The order of discussion should place a priority on needs of people and ministry before administrative items are covered. How a meeting begins determines the priority of the hour. Meeting needs of others is the priority of deacon ministry.

Enlisting Church Members

As ministries are developed, the church should be informed of their development. The pastor and staff can be a great assistance in this. As needed, church members should be allowed to volunteer for working with the deacons in various ministries. The degree of work and the number needed in each ministry will be dictated by the work attempted. It may be that a ministry fair where members can be informed and volunteer to assist is one way of including members in ministry to people in need.

One of the great benefits of a deacon ministry using spiritual gifts as the organizing principle to meet needs of the church and community is the model of ministry it provides for the church. God has come to indwell each believer and has gifted each one for ministry. The spiritual gifts are the point at which God's power intersects the needs of the world with His power through the lives of believers. Ministry, then, is the responsibility of the whole church and not just the responsibility of the deacons.

Developing deacon-led ministry teams, however, provides a model of ministry for the entire membership. As the church sees the deacons focused on ministry, members begin looking for opportunities to serve. As the church observes the deacons in the process of discovering and using their spiritual gifts, they begin to embrace gifts as the organizing principle for ministry. When the church sees the joy and power evidenced in the lives and ministries of the deacons, members will seek the same joy and power in their own lives and their own ministries.

Resourcing Deacon-led Ministry Teams

Deacon-led ministry teams require resources to prepare them for ministry and to provide the necessary elements for conducting specific ministries. Resources for *general spiritual preparation* should be provided. Leaders have a bounty resources available— in print, through on-line avenues, podcasts. It is not possible to narrow down a list.

To assist members of the congregation in discovering their spiritual gifts, their grace gifts, we can recommend the companion piece to this deacon resource. *Gifts of Grace* by Charles Garner and Tony Martin helps believers identify their spiritual gifts, understand biblical guidelines for using gifts, and identify specific ministries for them to explore related to their gifts. This would help members better understand how they can line up their gifts and calling with the teams formed by the deacons.

Specific resources for various ministries must also be provided. These include study materials, skill-development resources, space, budgetary support, supplies and other such resources needed to conduct specific ministries.

For instance, one pastor equips his Hospital Ministry Team by giving each deacon a New Testament with passages of comfort marked for ease of use. The pastor also mentors each deacon on the team until he feels comfortable in the ministry. One church with a Grief Ministry Team supplies the team with booklets related to the grief process. These are secured for the team from a local Christian book store and presented to the family as the team ministers to them.

In many instances, deacons provide for ministry needs from their own resources, but in some instances, the church can provide necessary budgetary resources to support the ministries. One church has a Ministry of Caring Team. This team accepted responsibility for painting and repairing some of the houses of the elderly and poor in their community. The church funded the supplies for their ministry.

Two interesting aspects of ministry are connected to this team. Only a three deacons composed the leadership of this ministry team. These have enlisted over 35 other members of the congregation to participate in the ministry. Also, a local paint supplier noticed that the men were charging different colors and types of paint to the church's account. Curiosity gained the upper hand of the store manager. When the manager learned that the men were painting the houses of the elderly and poor in the community at no charge, she committed to supply the paint free to the team for every house they painted.

Trust that God will guide you to and provide for you the resources necessary to do the ministries He has led you to do.

Notes and Observations

Notes and Observations

Session 9
Becoming a Team

Keith Wilkinson

By the time the Apollo 13 space mission approached lift-off, the interest of the American people had waned from the earlier space flights. Space travel was fast becoming common place. People took note, but the news quickly assumed "page 6" status in most newspapers. Yet, Apollo 13 soon riveted attention as no space flight had before or perhaps since. An explosion tore away part of the space craft and the crew suddenly faced the prospect of dying in space, adrift though the universe.

Back on earth, the news jolted people into action. Churches filled with people who prayed for the crew. In Houston, the support crew went into feverish activity to solve the problems. As one problem was solved, another life-threatening one emerged. Together they worked out repairs, dreamed up innovative approaches and coached the crew in how to solve problems. In short, both space crew, ground crew, and in a larger sense, the entire nation became part of a team dedicated to the safe return of the astronauts.

Teamwork might be a familiar concept, yet it is one that is often overlooked when it comes to tasks in the church. We are accustomed to seeing teams at work in sports, for example. In football, basketball, and countless other sports, we discuss the various strengths and weaknesses of our favorite teams and their opponents. We observe, that often, the best team does win! In making teamwork happen, a sports team gains strength, momentum, and single-minded purpose that gives them advantage.

Teamwork is a familiar concept in American history. Even the most rugged frontiersmen understood what it meant to have the support of others. People would come together for "barn raisings" and for mutual defense. Teamwork even built churches in those earlier days.

Teamwork is a familiar concept for today's church leaders. Church members might not always understand the subtleties of organizational charts and job responsibilities but most comprehend what it means to be part of a team. When the ministry of deacon service is described in terms of teamwork, it is easier for most persons to understand. Ask me to serve as a deacon and I might easily feel overwhelmed and inadequate. Ask me to become a part of a team of deacons, I immediately sense that I am part of something important. I sense that I will not *be* alone nor *work* alone. Being on a team gives confidence. Team members believe that they will be "coached" by one another.

Through teamwork, deacons find that they can serve with effectiveness.

How do we become teams?

Team building has eight attributes.

1. Participative leadership

Teams are not dictated into being. Leaders must participate in the team-building process. In sports, coaches get onto the field among the players in the practice sessions. They talk about plays, but they also show how things are done. Team *builders* participate in team *building.*

2. Shared responsibility

Teams work out shared responsibilities. Unlike hierarchical

organizations, team members have some part in one another's work. Teams work together and share responsibilities.

3. Alignment of purpose

Perhaps the most important aspect of team building concerns the purpose of the team. Teams can be built when there is a singleness of purpose. Everyone's attention must be focused in the same direction. Otherwise, teams break down and become simply collections of individuals.

4. Effective communication

Building teams requires communication. Teams must know what they are about, what plans are being worked, or what problems need solution. Provide potential team members all the relevant information you have at your disposal.

5. Future focus

Teams are built with a focus on the future. What is the future toward which your team is striving? In sports, that future might be to win the next game. In deacon service, that future might be to meet specific needs or to build the church's outreach and ministry in the community.

6. Task oriented

Teams focus on specific tasks that will enable them to realize their future. Each team member should understand what tasks must be done and how to do them.

7. Creative talents

Each team member brings certain creative talents to the team experience. Teams are built when opportunity exists for each person's creativity to flow into the team enterprise.

8. Rapid response

Teams learn flexibility and make rapid responses to problems and challenges that face them. In building teams, leaders must respond quickly to challenges.

Recently, a group of people met for a retreat at the Christian camp facility. After intensive sessions of study and problem-solving, the group met at the ropes course. After receiving instructions, each participant had to be learn to tie rope harnesses, walk a tight wire to a stand. There they scaled the stand to be attached to a pulley on a high wire that descended to a large tree some thirty yards distant.

For most of the middle-aged men in the group, the prospect of sailing down a high wire incline was intimidating. But one by one, they began the process. Rope harnesses were tied and inspected. The group began to laugh nervously and to tease one another. Walking the first tight wire, though not far off the ground, was not as easy as it looked. Balancing on the wobbling wire took some doing. Again, the group began to coach one another and to encourage the ones having difficulty. Scaling the stand was not too hard, but it took exertion. Looking down from the stand was another matter. A skilled camp staff member explained what to do. He pointed out group members at the bottom of the descent who would catch the descending person to keep him from crashing into the tree at the other end.

Quickly, each person realized just how much trust was involved. Could I trust my harness to keep me attached? What about the hook and pulley? What about the camp staffer's instructions—did he really know it would work? And what about my colleagues at the bottom of the descent? Would they really be able to catch me and prevent injury? Could I really trust it all?

Maybe, I should turn around and descend the stand as I had come up. The only thing I knew for certain was that I could trust myself.

The decision was made to trust the people and the equipment. Jumping from the stand, the harness tightened and the pulley descended the wire. A squeal from somewhere in boyhood emerged as I descended. My colleagues managed to catch my propelling body and saved me from being impaled by the tree. On solid ground, I felt triumphant. I had indeed done it! More importantly, I felt part of the team!

What had I learned about team building on those ropes and wires at this camp? I experienced first hand six key elements of team building.

1. Trust building

I had to trust my instructors and the staff who had put together the adventure course. Building teams starts with building trust. I knew that the camp had been doing the adventure course for some time. They had experience. Teams build trust on shared experiences. One of the best trust building experiences is to share a retreat experience together that involves trust building activities.

2. Goal setting

Our goal was simple: to get up on the stand and descend the high-wire without getting injured or killed! All of us knew what the goal was. Everything we did was designed to help us accomplish that goal. Teams work best when they work off of particular goals. Deacons should set specific goals for what they are trying to accomplish, then, build teams to accomplish the goals. The clearer the goals the better.

3. Challenge/stress

The challenge and the stress that accompanied our ropes course effort were essential ingredients in our team-building process. Teams don't become teams without a challenge. Perhaps the challenge for your deacon team-building comes from serious problems in your church's fellowship. No one likes to face difficulty, but difficult situations can be turned into positive challenges.

4. Peak experience

Teams come together when they share a peak experience. If teams are formed for visiting church members, it is the actual visit that makes the experience. If the team's responsibility is to help a family in crisis, the experience of garnering that support makes it a peak experience.

5. Humor/fun

Our climbing a stand only to go careening down a high-wire was serious business for each of us. No one wanted to get hurt. Yet, it was the humor that emerged from the group that made it all possible. We poked fun at ourselves. We teased one another about the quality of our knot-tying. Walking the first wobbly wire made for some funny moments by otherwise dignified people. We dropped our dignity and our masks—and became a group of kids once again.

Teamwork ought to be fun! You'll know that teamwork is taking hold when team members start laughing and having fun together. Recently, I told a group of leaders, "You'll know that you're doing a good job in your Sunday School classes when people walking down the halls hear laughter coming from your classroom. Bible study can be and should be fun!" How long has it been since you laughed in church? In deacons' meetings?

6. Problem solving

One of our group had trouble tying his ropes to make the harness. Two or three began to help him and before long the problem was solved. Solving problems is perhaps the highest form of teamwork. No situation in life really lends itself to a "cookie-cutter" solution. Church life is no exception. As deacons, you will be called on to solve new and complex issues in your church's life and ministry. Each ministry action you take presents new problems for you to solve. Working as a team, problems will be confronted and solutions found. As each problem is addressed, the team develops new skills and becomes able to face new problems and challenges.

Synergism

The end result of teamwork is **_synergism_**. Teams bring together the energies of many people and unite them into a single effort. The synthesis of such energy is called synergism. That's a technical word for the idea that we are all stronger and smarter than any one of us alone.

Guidelines for Team Leaders

Here are some guidelines for being successful in team leadership:

1. Learn your communication style.

What are your strengths and weaknesses? How well do you get along with people who have styles different from yours? Some communicate in generalities and paint the big picture. Others communicate using details, focusing on a specific part of the picture. Some prefer to stick with facts and figures. Others talk about feelings and intuitions. The best teams have a mixture of communication styles. A leader should learn his own particular style.

2. Learn the team members communication styles.

What are their strengths and weaknesses? Which ones are likely to blend well with yours? Where is friction likely to occur? How can those frictions be eased?

3. Develop acceptance of authority.

No one has more authority over others than they are willing to grant. Team leadership involves understanding one's own authority and meshing it with the acceptance of the team.

4. Expect good performance.

To get the best results, the team leader should expect the team members to perform. A team's members become accountable to one another. Don't be afraid to raise issues of accountability. The team should state expectations and ask members how they are doing in performing according to those expectations.

5. Make team meetings productive.

Don't waste people's time. Don't meet unless needed. Set an agenda and stick to your time frame. If discussion continues too long, say, "We have agreed to meet only until 8 p.m. Let's move ahead to the next agenda item." Summarize discussions and action plans. Bring closure to decisions.

6. Communicate.

Keep everyone informed about what is happening. Stay on top of details. Ask questions.

7. Build consensus.

Consensus is not necessarily voting or majority rule. Consensus reflects the agreement of everyone to support team decisions. If anyone disagrees, you have not yet arrived at a consensus. Consensus building takes longer, but in the long run, it is worth the time.

8. Create a positive climate.

Lead by example. Encourage people. Don't participate in or condone blaming, belittling, or complaining. Help team members appreciate one another's strengths and overlook their weaknesses. As the leader, believe in the process that team building provides.

Celebrate

Teams celebrate! Each victory is cause for rejoicing. Celebrate victories whenever and wherever they occur. If it is the team's first effort at visitation, celebrate it. Share the results. Talk about what has happened. Affirm the team and its efforts. Nothing motivates quite like success. Give a few high fives. Pat each other on the back. Say, "Good job." Tell the church. It will do the Body good to see a joyful celebration of work well done.

Evaluate

How will you know when you have built a team? Believe me, you will know. Here are some things that might give a clue:

You'll know you are a team when…

- you can't wait to see your team members.

- you look forward to your next activity together.

- you see things begin to happen.

- you can't believe that you did it.

- you sense that you are actually working on something worthwhile.

- you see how what you are doing fits your church's mission.

- you start recruiting others to be on the team with you.

Following Jesus' example:

Jesus didn't just teach about teamwork—He lived it. From the beginning of His public ministry, He surrounded Himself with a diverse group of disciples and patiently formed them into a ministry team. His example offers profound insight for deacon ministry today.

- He called people to join Him (Mark 1:16–20). Jesus invited people into shared purpose—ordinary individuals with different backgrounds and temperaments. He didn't build a staff; He built a team.

- He shared life with them (Luke 8:1–3). Meals, travel, worship, and rest were all part of their shared journey. Much of their learning happened in the in-between moments, not just in formal teaching.

- He gave responsibilities (Luke 9:1–6; 10:1–20). Jesus trusted His followers with meaningful tasks, sending them out two by two. He delegated power and authority, then brought them back for reflection and learning.

- He held them accountable (Mark 9:33–37). When disputes or failures arose, Jesus corrected them with grace and instruction. He didn't gloss over problems—He used them as growth moments.

- He mentored individuals (John 3 with Nicodemus; John 21 with Peter). Some of His most transformational ministry was one-on-one. As a team leader, He saw what each person needed and shaped His approach accordingly.

- He cultivated unity (John 17:20–23). In His prayer for His disciples—and for those who would come after—Jesus focused on unity. He didn't ask for uniformity, but for shared heart and mission.

- He modeled servanthood (John 13:1–17). On the night He was betrayed, He washed His disciples' feet. The basin and towel became His credentials. *"I have set you an example,"* He said, *"that you should do as I have done for you."*

Jesus built a team of transformed people who became world-changers—not because they were perfect, but because they were faithful and empowered by the Spirit. Deacons are called into this same pattern: to build trust, foster unity, share responsibility, and reflect Christ in service.

So continue to:

- Pray for the people your team will touch.

- Pray for your team.

- Pray for unity—teamness.

- Pray for being one with God through Jesus Christ.

- Pray for the world.

Being on God's team is what serving God is all about.

Notes and Observations

The Challenge

"The way to greatness is through the dust."

Jesus' words to the disciples came not at a moment of triumph but at a moment of tension—when power and prestige had begun to creep into the hearts of even His closest followers. James and John had asked for seats of honor. The others were indignant. Jesus, instead of rebuking them, called them together and redefined greatness. Not by might. Not by office. Not by recognition.

"Whoever wants to become great among you must be your servant (diakonos), and whoever wants to be first must be slave of all. For even the Son of Man did not come to be served, but to serve, and to give His life as a ransom for many."

—Mark 10:43–45

This is the heartbeat of the deacon. Not to ascend a ladder, but to descend into service. Not to wear a title, but to carry a towel. Not to direct others from above, but to lead from within, shoulder to shoulder, through the dust of real ministry.

The Call to the Dust

The name *diakonos* was never a title to be worn—it was a path to be walked. In the ancient world, the *diakonos* was one who kicked up dust behind him in a hurry to serve. He was the one who showed up when others turned away. He was the one who showed up when others turned away. She was the one who, like Phebe—the *diakonos* of the church at Cenchrea—saw need, heard pain, and stepped toward it, not away. Their footprints marked the pathways of grace.

That same trail now lies before you.

In the quiet corners of the sanctuary and the noisy chaos of the community, in the hospital waiting room and the kitchen of a single mother, you are the presence of Christ—not because you bear a title, but because you bear His image, His Spirit, and His towel.

The Call to Multiply

But this calling is not yours alone to carry. You have been entrusted not only with service—but with leadership in servanthood. You are not just called to serve—you are called to form, equip, and guide others into service. You are to create ministry teams, empower others to use their gifts, and organize the fellowship of believers into a functioning, living Body of Christ.

You are the "gravity" that helps the gifts of others find their orbit.
You are the spark that ignites quiet potential.
You are the bridge between a willing heart and a real-world need.

The Call to the Cross

Let us be clear: this calling is costly. There will be days when you are misunderstood, unthanked, or unnoticed. There will be times when the basin is heavy, and the towel feels worn thin. But this is the way of the Cross—and the way of the Kingdom.

Jesus washed feet that would flee.
He fed people who would betray.
He carried a cross that wasn't His.

He did all of it in love—and all of it as a servant.

144

"Have this mind among yourselves, which is yours in Christ Jesus, who, though He was in the form of God, did not count equality with God a thing to be grasped, but emptied Himself, by taking the form of a servant (diakonos)..." —Philippians 2:5–7

You are now called to reflect that same mind, to embody that same path.

The Invitation

So, dear deacon—dear servant through the dust—this is your challenge:

Lead with a basin, not a baton.

Serve not from obligation, but from overflow.

Build teams that reflect the Body, not just your image.

Call out the gifts in others as you discover your own.

Let your joy be found in obedience, not applause.

Be first in love, last in recognition.

And never forget: the way to greatness is still through the dust.

You are not alone. You are part of a fellowship of servants, scattered across churches and communities, walking in the steps of Jesus. May the Spirit of God empower you, may the Word of God guide you, and may the love of Christ compel you.

Now go—and serve.

Consider the companion resource to help your church members discover their spiritual gifts and ministries.

Gifts of Grace
Discovering and Using Your Spiritual Gifts
Larry Garner & Tony Martin

You were made for ministry.

God has given every believer spiritual gifts—grace gifts—to empower ministry and reflect His presence in the world. *Gifts of Grace* is a practical and biblically grounded resource that helps Christians identify, understand, and use those gifts effectively. Through Scripture-based teaching, a personal gifts inventory, and real-life application, this resource equips individuals and church groups to grow in spiritual maturity and fulfill their calling.

Whether you're exploring spiritual gifts for the first time, seeking deeper purpose, or leading others in their discovery, this book offers a clear and accessible path toward Spirit-empowered service in and through the Body of Christ.

Ideal for:
- Personal study and reflection
- Small group or Sunday School use
- Church leadership and ministry team development

This study will inspire and equip you to live as a steward of God's grace.

Available at Amazon, Barnes & Noble, and national retailers.

Beyond Expectations
The Kingdom No One Expected

What kind of Kingdom begins with a cross?
Jesus came preaching the Kingdom of God—but not the one anyone expected.

Beyond Expectations invites readers into 55 vivid vignettes—each a devotional window into the surprising nature of Jesus' reign. From Cana's joy to Calvary's cry, these reflections explore a Kingdom not built on conquest but compassion, not rooted in might but mercy.

Blending pastoral warmth, poetic insight, and biblical depth, this devotional theology brings Scripture to life in ways both reverent and real.

Perfect for personal devotion or group study.
Step into the Kingdom. Let it turn your expectations upside down.

Profiles from Paul
A Life Poured Out for the Kingdom

What Jesus began, Paul explained and extended.

In *Profiles from Paul*, 75 reflective vignettes trace the apostle's journey—from Damascus to Rome, from church planter to prisoner—rooted in Acts and the Epistles.

Each entry weaves together biblical narrative, historical insight, original poetry, and thoughtful questions for reflection. Accessible and engaging, this book is written for everyday believers seeking clarity, encouragement, and spiritual growth.

Whether for devotion, study, or leadership development, *Profiles from Paul* invites readers to walk the path of faith with Paul as their guide.

Available at Amazon, Barnes & Noble, and national retailers.